THE GOSPEL OF
FURY

THE GOSPEL OF
FURY
THE WORLD OF MAKE BELIEVE

Dedicated to God
Written by I. B. Fury
Proofed by Redemption
Edited by Faith

First Edition 2016

WESTBOW
PRESS®
A DIVISION OF THOMAS NELSON
& ZONDERVAN

WestBow Press books may be ordered through booksellers or by contacting:

WestBow Press
A Division of Thomas Nelson & Zondervan
1663 Liberty Drive
Bloomington, IN 47403
www.westbowpress.com
1 (866) 928-1240

ISBN: 978-1-5127-7199-2 (sc)
ISBN: 978-1-5127-7201-2 (hc)
ISBN: 978-1-5127-7200-5 (e)

Library of Congress Control Number: 2017900616

Print information available on the last page.

WestBow Press rev. date: 1/30/2017

CONTENTS

PART 3. THE PARABLES OF FURY 167

PART ONE

The Archangel

SECTION I

The Passage of the First Epoch of Humanity

ON FRIDAY, JUNE 3, 2016 THE ARCHANGEL OF THE FIRST EPOCH OF Man turned fifty-three years old.

For his entire lifetime on earth angel Fury had been anticipating his understanding of God's modern message. God's intent and purpose had indeed become clear and could not be ignored.

Fury now understood the great potential of God's desire, along with the clear message man needed for His mission. The Gemini Star signaled its arrival, and Fury began writing the modern word in 2015.

Thanks to God's intelligent design, and His power over creation, Fury was provided all the keys contained within his one life that any angel would need to fulfill an earthbound mission to deliver needed knowledge to man. To fail God, to fail family, to fail mankind; none of these were possibilities for the messenger of the epoch at this moment in man's history.

Two-thousand years of calendar time have now passed, and man and fate have arrived at the moment where the first epoch passes into the second. Those same two-thousand years of time passed across the entire globe of the earth and the world of faith; it made no difference what you believed in or if you maintained any belief at all. During this same two-thousand years of earth time, heavenly time has added up to just one month; heaven moves at the speed of light, while the earth calmly revolves around the sun.

God chose the passing of the epoch as the time to deliver this gospel containing the modern testament, and to include all of mankind as the target for His earthly mission. Two-thousand years ago the son of God walked the earth for thirty-three years of his life; two-thousand years ago the son was pinned to a wooden cross, and sent back to the Father. For two-thousand years of calendar time God's message of creation and salvation has been spread across the globe.

This modern testament is gospel that cherishes all years of history and belief, faith and knowing; targets every heritage and tradition as belonging to the one God, and wholeheartedly claims creation and salvation as the domain of God and heaven. Bring your skepticism and keep it near to your heart as it is golden; leave your sarcasm at the door because it is a waste of time and imagination.

At the beginning of 2015, Fury recognized that the pages of the book of fate had delivered him to the correct time, and with enough ability to provide the Archangel's message for the new epoch. Destiny had finally come close enough to view, and Fury recognized God's intent and purpose.

All men, women, and children with or without faith, and especially skeptics, should know that the modern testament has arrived on time; not to early, and not too late; right on time and according to heaven's plan. The entire world needs to understand that the Supreme Being has made the effort, and that the mission for the epoch has been sent at the turn of the epoch intentionally.

All the close and far corners of the world, each and every ethnicity of man, each and every conceivable religion, and every body still breathing should benefit in knowing the simple inclusive truth of the modern testament.

God, the Supreme Being, is reaching out to touch all of the people He shepherds to let them know that being united in freedom of belief is to know Him better and simply; this simplicity is the way He intends spirituality to emerge into progress.

Heaven and earth will exist closer for a time now, as the angel delivers the gospel truth into the reality of today's world. The chief angel of the mission maintains a family of angels around him, has God as captain, and has been provided many reasonable things needed in the modern world. Some of these things will be hard to believe, and even seem preposterous, possibly even shocking to consider, and some things may be too much to hope for. Be a good skeptic, and be a good judge.

This earthbound mission assigned to the archangel is no small task: just one man with one lifetime, tasked to reach all of humanity, to achieve God's desired goal in just one hundred-fifty years, to reduce the trend of doubt spreading across the globe by ten percent, seems like a lot to ask of one writer and teacher. Then again, God did provide the messenger and the tools for the mission, and God knows best.

Archangel is a heady title for a so-called messenger of God who comes straight out of the blue claiming to have the word of God for the whole planet. Archangel of the First Epoch of Mankind is even loftier. The titles used in the gospel are intended to explain things and to help you remember, to position the mission and story into reality, and to assist the gospel on it's way to becoming the established worldwide truth. The greater goal of global understanding can take generations to propound which is fine; for the greater glory of God's personal happiness and heaven's joy, there is no time to waste.

Even though there is one hundred-fifty years to reduce doubt by ten percent; now is the time to get started. The target goal is just ten percent globally, but there are almost five billion people in the world now; each one of those human beings has a soul coming from, or going back to, the Kingdom of Light. Yes, there is a lot of work to do in a short amount of time. Remember, one hundred-fifty years on earth is only two heavenly days; by the time things happen on earth, its old news in heaven.

Praise Him, love Him, don't forget to fear Him; don't abuse Him or take Him for granted, and above all don't ignore Him.

A world where humanity and heaven can be joined in legacy is at hand. The knowing angel will act decisively, and with precision; it remains up to mankind to provide the angel with what he wants to complete his quest.

Fury was passed to the earth through God's design and creation; being delivered to his parent's angel Faith and angel Understanding on June 3rd, 1963.

On June 3rd, 1963 Catholic Pope Saint John XXIII passed away returning through creation to heaven's gates, and the Kingdom of Light. Fury admits the Pope's passing as a marker for his own arrival, and he thanks God for the star, and for the key that helps unlock mystery.

Angel Fury's date of birth is one star of many stars that shed light onto God's modern story.

God provides keys and stars for His earthly missions. A key helps to make knowledge out of mystery, and a star is a signal from eternity. The mission in this case is these stories, delivered to provide knowledge of God's direction for freedom of worship, and a future of understanding liberty in praise.

As the shepherd of humanity, He will guide man's commitment to Him and enhance His direction as He desires and makes clear.

He is the shepherd, and He is the one God, and the Supreme Being. He will provide stories and learning for as long as we can keep on looking and listening. If we choose to ignore His message, and pass over His word, then we do so at our own peril.

God's keys and stars tie the Supreme Being's designs and creations into reality so that we see His intelligence, and can seek to understand His intent and purpose. Mankind has managed progress, and now creates and maintains the tools to shape his destiny along with his path toward God, and toward the heavenly stars.

At this time, the beginning of the new epoch, mankind has passed into his adulthood.

Mankind's intelligence remains obvious, and on display each day in the reality of time and challenges God and heaven. This story is gospel and exists as a rare mission sent into the world to balance God's intelligence with the intelligence of man, and to remind man the skeptic of His own being. Such reminders are necessary from time to time, and serve both heaven in eternity, and the earth which maintains mortal life and time.

At fifty some years old, Fury is now beyond the half way point of a human life. God's plan and Fury's creation, including his family and friends and our purpose, will be left for history, while the archangel and his company will be passed back to heaven and God before too long.

God's legacy is His to desire; His to create; His to nurture; His to cherish. Ultimately God's legacy serves the Kingdom of Heaven along with humanity and civilization. We are all God's children, and remain close to His breast in love where we belong. God's power of creation and His intelligent design provide Him with many religions to serve His needs, and to provide the world with a rich heritage. There are some things that are clearly designed to be special, and that includes the son of God. God will continue to want special things, until He decides He is done wanting special things. If the archangel says he can bring a special thing or things, then the archangel owns that upon his shoulders; between God and the angel some things exist in faith.

At the beginning of the second epoch of man, the archangel provides the strength of knowledge and the power of words in order to deliver God's message, to enhance understanding, and deliver knowing at this specific point in history.

The mark of the heavenly epoch is two thousand years. Two thousand earth years is the approximate equivalent of just one of heaven's months. So, the son of God was passed back to the Father roughly one heavenly month ago; not too long ago in heavens terms, longer in terms of God's earthly paradise and humanity's knowledge and experience with time.

From the first epoch of calendar time, and humanity's childhood, mankind now passes into adulthood, and this story acknowledges that passage, and serves to demonstrate the power of eternity, and solidify God's modern presence, and helps us examine His control over humanity through the generations.

Fury is chief angel of the mission which he named The Gemini Star. At this moment of the new millennium, and the beginning of the modern epoch, Fury may be the single mission angel to provide written prophecy.

Angel Fury's wife and knowing partner, angel Redemption, is a close witness to the eternal power passing into the world for this story. The Gospel of Redemption does make a good title for a story, so we shall see if she shares her written inspiration with mankind, or keeps it and her learning for God, and the kingdom. Either way, Redemption is at hand, and within mankind's grasp.

Each mission angel on earth could provide written insight into their existence, and the power of God and eternity in their lives. The compulsion to share God's word in modern times though is not ubiquitous, and reasonable men and women are complaisant enough to enjoy the paradise of earth as it exists, rather than to challenge reality with a modern view of belief. We shall see what we get. We will also witness in time if the Gospel of Fury stands out as a modern story explaining God's reality, or whether modern prophecy becomes fashion or ridiculous.

The success of <u>The Gospel of Fury</u> and the fulfillment of the legacy require mankind's belief in purpose today, and require the understanding that these stories are His tools to give Him what He wants. It is belief and understanding that turns heaven's plans into earth's reality today, tomorrow, and forever in heaven in eternity. Big dreams do require big plans.

The eternal legacy is tied to the reality of man's world; hand in hand the two grow into a united direction which is toward God and His happiness. The legacy that exists in the world then becomes reality for heaven in the end.

SECTION II

Your Judgment Day

ANGEL REDEMPTION SITS TO THE RIGHT HAND OF GOD, AND REMAINS present at each Judgment event in heaven. On the left hand of God sits the son of God. God, and the son of God are normally not present at Judgment, and this is the way you want it. A quiet Judgment Day enjoying your own passage into the freedom of heaven is a fine way to go.

You do not want God presiding over your Judgment Day. More importantly than that, you do not want God standing next to you offering His own testimony at your Day of Judgment.

Offending God or speaking on His behalf during mortal life are each decisions you can make that could result in having God standing next to you in your gallery at your Judgment. The rule of law belongs to man, and shapes civilization, and the progress of civilized society. God's single modern Commandment for man is to prevent persecution and suffering. Prevention of persecution and suffering is difficult to write into mankind's rule of law; we should keep that commandment upon our personal shoulders, and in our hearts as God describes in the apparent truth of this gospel.

Angels of God are His messengers, and willingly accept the weight of His words upon their shoulders as the purpose they serve. If you wonder how there is enough time for every single judgment day when there are billions of souls; if you wonder how God would have time for especially you; it is eternity, there is plenty of room and all of time, and you matter.

Angels on earth hope to bear the burden of learning with them to study their superpower during their lifetime. An angel's superpower is in its duty to God and beings. Angels study their superpower by struggling against it throughout their lifetime, so that upon returning to heaven they function more effectively in their heavenly capacity. An angel's basic function is as a messenger, an informed messenger is the better, an enlightened messenger is best of all, and most helpful.

Angels in heaven support events and emotions and character and actions and knowledge and adventure and everything in between, and anything you can imagine. The range of possible roles for angels to play is unlimited! You can understand this better by understanding that the grace of God is as broad as the bandwidth of light itself. An angel's duties, like His grace, have no limits; angels willingly and without complicity serve at God's desire, and serve being as well. Heaven functions, and functionality matters; beings function well when they function together willingly. That is God's intent and design.

Heaven is not the same as life, but heaven is just as good as dreaming. If you like to dream, then you will enjoy the perfection of heaven.

Angels on earth, who were not sent to live and learn, often do not live long.

Angels are not any more special than any other being in heaven. Some beings enjoy being, while other beings enjoy purpose in being; you can have whatever you want in the Kingdom of Light which is heaven. If you choose purpose, then you ask to work as an angel, and so it shall be.

As an angel, one heavenly day, you too may travel back into the world and life in order to learn and remember all the concerns of life, and the struggles life includes, while you study your superpower. Beings can come through creation to earth often, but heaven is compelling, and the struggles of life are not too often tantalizing. When God says you gotta go, though, you gotta go.

Angelic existence includes balanced learning because it inevitably involves teaching, and the best teachers are also good learners. Being a studious angel is as good a practice as being a studious human being.

God is all knowing, and His angels are His experts. God is the Supreme Being, and enjoys using His angels. You may also use His angels in your prayers for help. It may be that in your circumstance of need, the expert may help you focus on your problem, and increase your concentration, and therefore a resolution may be found readily at hand. But, don't thank the angel, thank God, since He sent the angel in the first place.

One heavenly day lasts for about one human lifetime of seventy-five years or so. Yes, there is a difference in the way time and being are measured on earth and in heaven.

Heaven exists and operates at the speed of light. A thinly layered administration of bureaucracy in heaven makes sense of existence, resolves every issue, and serves God's purpose.

Equivalency among beings balances the mechanics of light and being, so that all things function well together in the heavenly scheme of things.

Heaven's favorite sport does happen to be Judgment Day. The son of God, who loves every aspect of humanity unconditionally, does enjoy sport as much as any being. The son of God, though, seeks the knowledge and understanding that judgment provides for the bureaucracy of heaven, and God's kingdom. The son of God may never have any reason to offer testimony at judgment.

Some Judgment events are spectacular, and draw the Father, the son, and a throng of witnesses and onlookers. You do not want such a special Judgment Day. Cherish and nurture your Life Savings, live a good life, and then you will enjoy a quiet Judgment Day. A quiet Judgment Day is the best medicine.

You cannot wrong a being that loves you unconditionally; therefore the son of God will not be standing in your court seeking penance from you. Heaven is a compelling place, and Jesus is in demand; rather than taking pleasure in the sport of judgment, Jesus is more likely than not spreading himself over heaven in eternity studying being and truth and tracking progress in the world of time which is earth.

Mankind is an ever changing thing, and the son of God admires man and remains involved in man's future as God the shepherd shapes it. Man's destiny is still just at its beginning, and there is much work to do. Heaven in eternity exists tirelessly to shape the land of time into what God hopes for the future; though man maintains free will and anticipates destiny, so the path of the world and man is not a foregone conclusion. The future lies ahead of us beyond what we know; that is God's concern as the Shepherd of Humanity.

Life is the goal of the Shepherd and His universe. Human kind is both the most remarkable life, and the most desirable life in His universe. He does not waste what He creates. Take care of what He created, so that when you come back to Him, you can bring things that make Him and heaven happy. Remaining a successful contributor to existence is the goal of being. All beings belong to the one God, all beings represent His greatest value; the stars and entities of the universe are all designed to support the true purpose of reality which is life; eternity also serves to support life which includes beings, and your soul is included. Creation and salvation are the understood properties that God uses to balance existence at the level He enjoys the most. This includes togetherness; or as close as we can come to one another; bringing heaven and earth closer to one another in understanding is a basic tenet of this gospel.

The living breathing planet Earth is a jewel within His universe, but mankind is the shepherd of his own planet. God is the Shepherd of

Humanity. Man's ingenuity is infinite; man's understanding of the earth and the universe is critical; God created man and time with perfection so that man can shepherd the earth in perfect balance and harmony.

Love God, praise God, Fear God; take care of your planet, take care of one another.

The reality of heaven may sound incredible, but the reality of heaven awaits us all. This is God's promise for each of us; that promise is worldwide and ubiquitous, and remains the truth under every condition of humanity.

At the beginning of this new epoch, God will tether man to His being so that progress toward the stars and heaven keep God the Shepherd at the forefront of man's thoughts. You can not reason without thinking, and you are not thinking reasonably if you plan on leaving God out of your destiny.

God's generational power over creation insures the potential for timely reminders of man's duty to God, and God's oversight of man's progress. He can send a single life and mission to tell a story, and He can send a generation to change the course of history.

There is no power on earth that comes close to the power of eternity over the reality of time on earth. All of time exists within eternity forever. Part of playing in heaven includes playing with time. Imagine playing anywhere in time; visit any time, play for as long as you want in time, go back and forth in time, get stuck in time, be careful with time, don't get lost in time even though a comforting angel will find you and secure your path.

Being free and careless is your responsibility; thank God for angels who exist in heaven to keep you straight, and reasonable.

Life at times may be compelling, but heaven is perfect all of the time.

We are adult now, and we are learning more about the great science of the universe, and how matter, and light, and gravity, and energy coexist fluidly to provide calm and cataclysm. God is the creator of the universe, God is the Shepherd of Humanity; mankind and being are the goals; man's reasonability will arrive in understanding that He will bridge the gap between myth and certainty.

One little story at a time, spread out over time, and the Shepherd will be here to remind us, and to send His word, over and over and over again, so that we piece God's eternal existence into the reality of life in a universe centered around a simple thing known as being.

SECTION III

The Being at the Heart of the Sun

WE HAVE TO BE TAUGHT AND WE HAVE TO LEARN; TAUGHT TO LISTEN and taught to hear; taught to watch and taught to see. These things brought to you in these modern stories are things you need to learn. You dare not discount this mission, or these stories provided to you as modern gospel.

These gospel stories come from a pure heart; though it is the heart of Fury, the Being at the Heart of the Sun, Archangel of the First Epoch. These strong words and ideals are thrust to the world deliberately in order to make the world believe. This is indeed a rare opportunity to grasp purpose, and to provide for legacy.

Archangel Fury openly converts his birth date 6/3/63 into the number 666 writing the mark of the beast, and thereby acknowledging and admitting to a popular anti-Christ reference and coincidence. Anti-Christ refers only to Fury's understanding that he is not to be understood as Christ, the son of God reborn. Fury exists solely as a paltry messenger of God's word, assigned the mission of freeing the son from man's limits, and liberating God from man's impulse toward self destruction, now and forever.

God has provided tools in the shapes of keys and stars from creation to help mankind see the mystery of God clearer in the lighted truth of reality. He then combines the facts with historic circumstance, to help us know, and understand in order to accept the truth as it is presented to us. The time for you to work together closely to confirm the message is upon you. There is no redemption without acceptance; there is no reason to delay the progress of the mission. Study the consistency of the gospel in scholarly fashion, share the story with your wisest learners while they still live, and encourage the gospel's reasonable advance into the reality of the modern world.

These are the truths God has entrusted to the mission delivered through the Gospel of Fury: the son of God never required any condition for every man, woman and child to attain eternal salvation, and to achieve forgiveness at heaven's judgment as God has promised, and provided for each of us; that mankind is fully capable of his own divisiveness, and self-destruction, without using God's name in argument, or during the creation of wars. So, be grateful and don't deny anyone their right to heaven in eternity. Argue among yourselves as men, and fight wars as men; no longer argue in God's name, no longer fight wars or commit terror in God's name.

His desire to be perceived in goodness exists hand in hand with His desire to remove doubt.

The Gospel of Fury: The Gemini Star describes Fury as the true presenter of the true Holy Grail; that cup that every one of us shares that contains the bond between the Father and the son that provides forgiveness of all mortal sin, and promises eternal salvation for each human life as it passes. Elevating salvation in eternity and forgiveness for mortal sin back to the level of the everlasting bond that includes all human beings is one important message for the world provided through these stories.

Gospel truth is rare; so there will be enough value presented in these stories to create everlasting impressions and lingering questions. The mark of the first epoch, and the two thousand years of human history it contains, is time for celebration and reflection on what has been good, and what has been bad, and the potential for what dreams can become when enough of us believe in today's mission, and when people spread the word that there is prophecy again in the land.

The Gospel of Fury: The Gemini Star was driven into the reality of the modern world for sister-in-law and cousin angel Love, and an overwhelming desire to deliver happiness to her. Whatever God provides as compulsion to deliver His word, so be it. Faith in Him is wonderful, and whatever gets His word into the modern world remains virtuous. The fact that Fury wants Love happy is a matter of record. The fact that Fury wants God happy is also a matter of record. The fact that Fury desires God's mortal legacy leaves you something to consider.

The writing of The Gospel of Fury: The World of Make Believe is compelled out of an overwhelming desire to provide happiness and friendship to the newly found angel Hate who the Lord saw fit to bring into the life of Fury during 2014. It takes a lifetime of listening and watching to knowingly spot things God sends. The second story is compelled into existence out of love and admiration for angel Hate, who is currently twenty-eight.

The final chapter of the trilogy will be named The Gospel of Fury: Redemption, and will be delivered to simply reiterate the modern testament in gentler terms. Achieving redemption for mankind at the epoch only involves acceptance and understanding of two thousand years of the misuse of God's name in terror and war. Judgment has been rendered, and the world's experience in pain has already delivered the balance God required; redemption is the conclusion to ease the collective conscience of mankind.

The gospel stories of Fury are laid out for history then as Love, Hate, and Redemption.

Thinking in terms of ensuring delivery of His word, including necessary mortal compulsion to drive the words into the world of today, Fury thanks God, resolving that Love, Hate and Redemption made for good drivers as well as good nick names for each of the currently planned stories. Each of God's angelic messenger's purpose in life, along with the inspiration they provide, comes from Him, with their help of course, and belongs to Him and them together. In the end, the angels on earth will return to God one by one; as will we all, each of us included. Fury's role is to describe the real life messengers briefly, and confirm the facts related to their lives, that are stars that become keys, like bones within a skeleton. The thirteen named angelic messengers provided through His design and creation are here, and now near in life in 2016.

God's story remains His responsibility to propagate in the fashion and scope He desires. Each of His messengers can serve His purpose to the degree their eternal beings, and God's desire, provide for through heavenly inspiration. The men, women, and children who would believe today, may help to fulfill the legacy Fury sees, desires, and reveals for you in these stories. The meek and the powerful alike may have interest in how well the modern word is received. The future may contain something wonderful for the world to watch and admire as real time prophecy unfolds wings bathed in dreams and hopes. Fury willingly accepted what God gave as inspiration and compulsion; agreeing that men may need coercion and promise in order to deliver and receive powerful messages in a modern world that may want the word of God, but have difficulty recognizing it and believing in it.

Love God, praise God, fear God; don't make it too difficult; be prepared for the Father.

Angel Fury also accepts the sound of Fury I, Fury II, and Fury III, in addition to Love, Hate, and Redemption. Fury's plan is to have the stories delivered in 2015, 2016, and then in 2017. Fury's mission as described in The Gemini Star would then be complete. The future is uncertain, though, and nothing is written in stone; it might turn out that the future will provide a path that destiny has not yet revealed for the book of fate; writing truth in the realm of spirituality may reveal that reality may turn out stranger than fiction.

The quest will be realized, abandoned, and may be forgotten as the angels of the mission age out, and are returned to the gates of heaven and God. Fury quips with his wife angel Redemption, "Imagine, returning to heaven and God trying to explain that mankind did not even notice."

Fury sometimes felt sickened with the prospect of failure; imagining he wanted his mortal life to end sooner rather than later. He sometimes felt so useless and tired of waiting and wanting that he even hoped his soul would be put to rest for the final time upon his eventual return to God. Can you imagine wishing for your final oblivion? Imagine reaching the point where even the promise of the Kingdom of Light and heavenly perfection could not offer solace; that the thought of the warm embrace of God Himself could not evoke hope for a happy existence in heaven. Bridging together heaven and earth seemed like it was taking an eternity while mortality remained scattered across a globe that was growing by leaps and bounds, but appeared unprepared to receive God's recurring words; yet over and over they must come; time after time, the Father will continue to amaze and confound in ways designed to bridge the gap of time and eternity to clear up mystery.

Fury would not fail God though. Fury did not believe the men of the epoch would lead mankind into failing God either. Fury knew the mission would succeed because delivery of the stories was his purpose, and that remained in Fury's control. Man's actions during Fury's lifetime would only prevent God's happiness if Fury's words were committed to ashes and digital oblivion. Fury could not know with certainty whether God truly would achieve an earthly legacy to match the mortal feelings and heavenly urges he thought he understood.

Choice and action are real enough; not to take action is choice enough to cause results intended and understood or not. Fury knew full well that God would accept inaction as action; God had forever to shape the world of life and time into what He intended would be our earthly paradise that will serve both man and heaven. God's own disappointment when known by mankind could actually become His happiness when the tide turns, and it always does.

Modern man has to be taught to listen, taught to watch, and taught to learn; taught to know what to know. The purpose of the modern message is to demonstrate God's power and intelligence. He sent the archangel, and named him Fury out of cause, not out of accident.

God has the luxury to watch our future become our destiny, and watch as destiny fills the pages of fate with those things He designed and created, similar to an artist who plans for the best outcomes. It is for God to know if the outcome of His planning matches His needs closely enough in an imperfect world where man maintains free will. We are created in His own image, so truly disappointing Him is improbable. God's judgment and our need for redemption remain intertwined in resolution that is inevitable when the tide eventually rises, and it always does.

Love God, praise God, fear God; enjoy the rising of the Sun each and every day.

SECTION IV

God's Design and Intelligence

FURY WILL HELP MANKIND ALONG THE PATH TOWARD BELIEF IN THE modern message. The ideal situation exists now as the Archangel of the First Epoch is placed into the world at just the right moment to show God's clever design and intelligence through His power over creation. Through the actions of God, the Supreme Being, and the clear words of the archangel, all of mankind can see the light of His reality through reason, exist in hope for the future, become filled with desire for understanding, and remain gladdened in knowing.

Uniting mankind's direction to God in modern belief and knowing is in no way designed or intended to replace tradition and heritage in spiritual worship and religious practice. Mankind is free to choose his form of belief. Mankind is not free to deny heavens acceptance of every human being who passes. There is no corner of humanity that will be denied entry through heavens gates. Jesus came on his mission and provided acceptance for each and every one of us; even without knowing, we are welcome; only oblivion results in any risk to the soul, yet even the oblivious can be fixed at the gates; God does not waste what He creates.

There is no need to harbor a fearful image of Hades that was indeed vanquished long ago. Do not imagine a Hades that includes a home for half of God's humanity. Do not try to imagine or worry about the things that Hades contains. The things Hades contains are for God to manage.

Do not confuse His love for every one of us with doubt in His goodness that always included everyone.

God's business is being, and cherishing being is our purpose. Taking care of being, and building life savings are our earthly role. Going back to God and the promise of heaven is the natural outcome of life; He designed and guided your life and looks forward to seeing you again, each and every one.

Fury has every mortal life on his side of God's modern message, because Fury has death on his side of the equation. There is just a little clarity required during life so that heaven runs a little smoother. No one is trying to take anything away from man in these modern stories, or make any really big changes, just a little tweaking and understanding is asked for. God will then feel newly known, newly respected, and even anticipated in the future. Mankind will know His modern touch, that He maintains feelings, and that He will maintain balance.

No mortal life is spared in passing; death is coming for everyone. The son's promise of salvation and forgiveness was always intended for every man, woman, and child who ever existed.

Fury enables a message that will provide spiritual treasures requiring faith and belief in addition to facts that are God's keys and stars coming from heaven to help man unlock God's mystery and respect the modern word in the light of intelligent design.

There were stars to be seen that presented plenty of keys to unlock mystery before Fury had ever been born; recognizing those stars and using heaven's keys took Fury a lifetime of learning before Fury could see the big picture. God did prepare the design, and then did the creating to deliver the guidance so the paltry angel would deliver the apparent mission. All that mankind has to do is be willing to piece it all together into global understanding, and then with a broad degree of acceptance the not so paltry archangel will be free to pursue his perceived quest, and deliver God's legacy.

Fury knows to include things in the gospel that man will recognize and want so the story provides truth and facts in order to balance belief and understanding into the semi certainty of knowledge; until the time we each pass away, though, truly knowing may always require an ounce of faith.

Existing as a human being, and therefore skeptical by nature, angel Fury himself understood the modern need to not only provide spiritual truth, but include factual coincidence and circumstance so the story would achieve balance in order to create a proper degree of interest, and become convincing enough to prove up God's presence. Fury hoped that a more scientifically minded man would be willing to recognize basic truths from life, and would admire prophecy that bridged God to one mortal life existing within a presentation of intent and planned purpose.

Mankind deserved manners, respect, and a gentle touch. The temptation for an angel to provide a too much spiritual influence would undoubtedly prove fool hearty and potentially discourage interest. Twisting history written into fate already while painting possibilities for the future to the correct degree would require care and guidance. God had provided some of that care and guidance through the life of the angel on earth Redemption.

Fury and Redemption are first cousins, designed that way and created that way out of the necessity of proximity so their comet like lives would collide in marriage and family. Whereas Fury was volatile, brash, and prone to emotional swings of mood; Redemption was calm, rational and much more realistic in her approach to life. Their partnership would provide the path to success to whatever degree mankind was willing to carry it during their lifetimes. As long as Fury's words were not lost, then God's mission would be a success. It was Redemption who viewed the initial words with her careful eye on simplicity and clarity which is what God wanted for spirituality and belief and knowing Him easily.

It is man's choice to ignore God's message while it was being delivered, but in passing, everyone becomes a believer. When you arrive at the gates of heaven you may ask if you are at the right place. What do you imagine will be the response? The response will be welcoming for each and every one. Interestingly enough, one heavenly gate serves all. After you pass through heaven's gates your life savings do remain with you, and take on special meaning and practicality for your heavenly pursuits throughout eternity. Heritage, geography, tradition, teaching and learning all play their role in life's interests as well as in the Kingdom of Light. If everyone had the same things in life, and wanted the same things in heaven; then being would be boring; God does not like boring any more than you do.

Your soul is what matters to the good Lord; your soul is what will return to the good Lord. What you practice as spirituality in life helps you get through life, and provides for the basics of understanding and knowing that will help to keep your soul intact on its journey out of the world of time, and into eternal existence. That spiritual understanding and knowing stays with you and grows forever, but is not a license to heaven, and it is not any better or worse than any other spirituality or understanding and knowing; oblivion is riskier. Heaven's concern is wellbeing; wellbeing is for every being.

Fury, whose eternal resting place is at the heart of the Sun, fears dying a bitter man; Fury fears the shame of returning to God having failed on a simple mission while God has provided so much for man to grasp hold of and to recognize as His intelligent design. Fury's direction and understanding is to attach his life to as many stars and keys as could be made available to enable broad acceptance of a mission whose purpose was to bridge prophecy into popular ideas and culture wherever possible. God is clearly enjoying popularity, so attaching God's message to popular thinking is a good thing and clearly a good path.

Fury's fear is a good thing. Fury would ensure God's words would rise like a sword from the earth remaining sharp on both sides to cut cleanly in every direction. Fury was shown the sword of God rising from the earth that would be placed next to the crucifix that provided for the son's passage to the Father at the young age of thirty-three. Fury interlocked the two powerful symbols side by side, interconnecting them together forever into what is now labeled the Gemini Star. This created a single symbol containing the Christian cross together with the rising sword of God, which also resembles an inverted crucifix, into one specific design named the Gemini Star. The inverted Christian cross is a popular reference attached to the idea of an anti-Christ figure. Archangel Fury had been shown to pick up the sword of God, and symbol of the anti-Christ, and to imbed it into the earth planting it next to the cross of Jesus as one more tool to help solidify purpose into today's world through the use of symbolism.

The symbol now called the Gemini Star adorns the cover of each of the Gospel of Fury stories in one fashion or another. The simplest version of the star appears on the cover of The Gemini Star. A more elaborate version of the Gemini Star which includes a depiction of the star inside the Sun that also includes an outer ring containing twelve depictions each representing the super power of one of the twelve central mission angels is included on the cover of this story The World of Make Believe. Redemption will include the star along with redemptive themed artwork carrying the principal figures Redemption, Love, Hate, and Fury.

Fury admitted to man that man had two heavenly days, which is one hundred fifty earth years, to grow God's modern word into understanding. Mankind can work together spiritually, philosophically, and intelligently in order to reach God's prescribed goals for love and well being.

Heaven knows angel Doubt described the desire for a ten percent reduction in man's doubt in God's goodness in order to establish a trend that would result in success two thousand years from now.

Love Him, praise Him, and fear Him; agree the future matters for us all; heaven and earth.

The turn of the second epoch will be upon mankind in two thousand years, or one heavenly month from today in 2016. Liberty in belief and tolerance of spirituality will have become ubiquitous by that time; there will have been no religious wars since God is putting an end to any justification for spiritual and religious fighting. When God wants war; He will pit man against man; God never has a need to pit man against himself in order to foster belief. Fight your wars as men; don't put God in the middle in order to fight for your belief; God gave you words and argument; argue all you want since it is healthy when you also celebrate respect, and agree on difference.

Fury understood people's sensibilities, and Fury knew people would not want to reread a story filled with preaching and unpleasant words from any messenger. Fury desired for people to appreciate God's fresh story, and to embrace the message rereading it once or twice. The angel on earth hoped to experience progress in his lifetime while he was young enough to follow his dream. He wanted God to know progress, and to see man's willingness to acknowledge modern prophecy, and to accept its ongoing relationship with the shepherd including understanding that God would continually make His path into the world.

God's ongoing word will in all ways remain necessary to the world of man, and will always make the difference in man's success in reaching the goals set by God the shepherd; for earth and for heaven's sake.

SECTION V

God Delivers Stars and Provides Keys

KNOWING AND BELIEF DURING LIFE BELONG TO GOD, AND ARE ultimately shaped by God over time, while worship belongs to man. Yes, it is obvious that man is free to worship however he pleases, while understanding and admitting there is one God. God only asks for an open heart, and a measure of innocence; God will take care of the rest for each life as desired and needed.

It is God who creates each life, it is God who cherishes each life, and it is God that welcomes each life back in its passing. Creation belongs to God, life belongs to man, and being is shared equally within time on earth and heaven in eternity; for man to use God, spirituality, or religion, to divide himself or to fight or to commit terror is clearly wrong; arguing with respect is a good and mighty thing, and a good use of human intelligence.

It was up to Fury, along with his team of angels, to deliver God's message to the world in order to simplify belief for mankind and encourage modern understanding, so that adult man could turn to the new epoch living with renewed knowledge of God, the son, and the promised Kingdom of Heaven; a simple thing really, except the new epoch exists intelligently in the business of the digital age, and man may have difficulty noticing the message.

These gospel stories sound Eurocentric because Fury is American, and must write with the knowledge and perspective that is available. The message is for every corner of the earth, and matters to everyone; man and earth united toward God, and not divided among themselves; pretty basic stuff, for everyone. Ingenuity it will take; mastering the word no small thing is that (in Yoda speak).

You may wonder how a mortal man in mid life, with little background, gains the knowledge and then maintains enough nerve to call himself Archangel of the First Epoch in order to create and deliver God's powerful word into the world. How can a man do such a thing as speak for God? That takes a lifetime of searching and learning and following; above all, it takes God's own intelligence in design and creation, including His eternal ability to pave the path moment by moment, day by day, one step and word at a time.

Delivering the words requires the assistance of countless unknowing angels on earth, living with me, passing through my life daily. The kindness and support passed along through eternal guidance and the power of the Kingdom of Light, is a gentle touch as simple as a nod and a smile to demonstrate God's joy at progress within the moment.

God first creates and delivers the life, including His stars and keys to signal His intentions. Eternity plays its part over the entire lifetime, and then God provides the impetus to drive the message into the world with unrelenting emotional force.

Other than the force of God's eternal power over being, why would a modern man attempt to deliver His word into the land of the living? You may suggest that God's word is delivered out of praise, love and faith; I would agree it should or could be. Being driven by human emotion and feelings from mind and heart help as well, when God is planning for success, and failure is not an option. Imagine failing after generations of planning, birthing, paving paths, shaping knowledge and experience, and then not having any real compulsion to actually write the story. He is not above using the trickery of human emotion to achieve His purpose. Do not laugh at the notion of love and caring to create this compulsion. He designed and created the heart, and it remains His captive.

Love him, praise Him, fear Him; especially take joy in His cleverness.

In The Gospel of Fury: The Gemini Star, Fury simply alluded to much of the truth he was to deliver. In The Gospel of Fury: The World of Make Believe, Fury spells out the gospel clearly and truthfully. Removing ambiguity is the purpose of The World of Make Believe. Turning mankind toward belief, and the realization that the mission is real and does matter, is the purpose of the second story known as Fury II or Hate.

In heaven's version of time, it is just less than one month ago that calendar time began together with the coming of the son on his earthly mission. Two-thousand years of calendar time have now passed, and we have arrived at the changing of the human epoch. Man now moves from the first epoch into the second epoch from childhood into adulthood.

Angel Fury is not the creature who believes man will embrace the earthly mission wholly, and in time. Fury is more likely betting against man's ability to work together to deliver mortal acknowledgment of God's intelligence along with the fulfillment of His desire for earthly legacy. It is not in Fury's personality or role to deliver benevolence, pretend understanding, or to ignore man's divisive nature. Fury's purpose is simple; deliver the things man needs that God showed him to deliver; it is up to man to do right with those things. Ingenuity, intelligence, and unity together with spirit, directed toward appreciation, will sanctify the mission by admitting God's progressive intent and purpose for the world today and tomorrow.

When we were children, walkie-talkies were the highest degree of technology a child could hope to possess. Such dreams of actually owning a pair of walkie-talkies were far beyond the possibility of our household. The children of Understanding and Faith grew up in a frugal environment based on love and togetherness. Since that childhood, progress has unfolded at ever increasing exponential rates to the point where technology, communications, and even economics are providing mankind with the ability to offer happy life styles across the globe. The true age of progress is never ending; do not suppose or maintain that this is not the nature of the Supreme Being or that heaven would be left out of human progress.

We are created in His image by design out of the necessity of purpose; God's purpose is to share in the glory of the world, and shape the future; His path into the world is created intelligently so you would plainly see His progressive needs. Misunderstanding the good Lord, and assuming that He and His plans would remain with history in the past would be an incorrect assumption, and an apparent mistake.

Love God, praise God, fear God; give Him credit for anticipating progress, and planning for His modern understanding.

Progress is indeed inevitable, and a good thing; man evolves in ways including thought and technology. Heaven and earth together belong to humanities great journey; the great journey was always part of the plan. Maintaining flexibility and remaining open to new understanding is one of the things we must practice in order to grow according to God's progressive needs. Morals and morality are large concerns, but largely the concern of man; God has a universe to maintain, heaven knows. Man has opportunity to worry for himself, and codify under the rule of law those bad behaviors as man sees fit. Individuality is vital; breaking the law is wrong; judging your fellow man and his behavior in God's name is always misguided.

SECTION VI

God's Holy Grail and the Bond with the Son

GOD LOVES MAN, BUT NOT AS MUCH AS THE SON LOVES MAN. THE Supreme Being is God of the universe, and all things in the universe. Mankind is one of the many things God loves within His universe. The son of God loves man completely and unconditionally. The son sees his father in mankind, as mankind is created in the Father's image. The son loves his father just as any child loves and cherishes a parent. This is common knowledge and beloved thought and understanding in the Kingdom of Light. God in turn loves the son as much as any father loves his children. God loves most things in the universe as well.

Now, the son loves man so much that he looked after mankind in a special way long ago. The son of God is blessed of course, and maintains impressive knowledge concerning the vitality of being as it exists eternally, as well as in the world of the living. Such knowledge and experience as the son maintains enables his insight into the needs and desires of the Father. After all, he is the son of God, and knows a lot about his father and the Kingdom of Heaven and how things work best. Heaven's best interests are in the best interest of each and every one of us beings. So, it was natural for the son to think logically about heavenly operations, and to walk in the footsteps of the father to make things work better for everyone.

Equivalence is the key to eternity, and the power of light. Mortal beings must regain equivalence upon returning to the Kingdom of Heaven and lighted existence. Without equivalence, heaven would not function properly, and God will not have heaven functioning improperly. There is plenty of impropriety in reality, so heaven is reserved for propriety. Unequal things do not work well at the speed of light. Unequal things are awkward things. Unequal things do not get along at all. Heaven could not be heaven without the propriety that equality provides.

Judgment Day is not just an afterthought or fun activity or heavenly busywork; Judgment Day is a managed spiritual requirement performed in order to reestablish heavenly equality among beings. Without equivalence the Kingdom of Heaven could not function as a successful bureaucracy. Without equivalence, things moving about at the speed of light would quickly become chaotic, and we know God is not the God of chaos, unless He desires and creates it. He did not create heaven to be chaotic, or even to be complicated. Neither God nor the son ever intended for knowing forgiveness and belief in salvation to be complicated for mortal beings who struggle with even the basics of life.

The eternal son of God has always watched over mankind, and could see that surviving mortal life, albeit in God's paradise on earth, included suffering and much struggle. The son of God did accept that many of the decisions mankind would make would always be based on the need to maintain life, and also that many of life's decisions would be based on emotions that had been created out of the image of the Father. Considering the circumstances of human life, the son made an important decision to act.

The son of God loves man, and asked his father if all men, women and children could be forgiven for the sins they committed while they toiled and struggled through life's circumstances. The benevolent Father understood where the son was heading with his notion. The Father agreed, knowing that judgment and equivalence were imperative in any event.

God together with his son then entered into their eternal bond, which existed before the son ever came into the world of man on his sacred mission. The mission the son of God took into the world of man began just about one heavenly month ago. Through the eyes of mankind, the entire first epoch of two thousand years has now passed. Mankind has created his fate, and developed our modern world of today. It remains His earthly paradise to shepherd; filled with the heavenly grace that we see and share daily; including the struggles some of us live with, just hoping we will survive to see the sunrise again.

The really special thing about human beings is our individuality. It is our individuality that is crafted especially by each of us, and takes a lifetime to create. The things we cherish the most from our lives are what is kept with us to become part of our life savings. These life savings belong to our soul forever, and remain deep inside our being so that we maintain continuity and personality between heaven and earth.

Without continuity and personality, God's heavenly perfection would exist in blurred vision, and there would be no understanding. Without continuity and personality, heaven would be pointless; God does not design and create intelligence only for it to remain pointless; life savings are the core of your being after you die, which are your functional contributions that are meaningful to God and heaven. Heaven is not simply a nice idea; heaven is a meaning-filled existence that serves the greatest purpose in a universe that has many sides.

God values perspective throughout His universe and this includes your opinion. Your opinion and perspective are important and will remain relevant inside your being throughout your mortal and heavenly existence. Your uniqueness gives God, the Supreme Being, His great joy. That is part of the value you bring to God.

There is no purpose served when cookie cutter lives are gathered into His presence; He did not create His own paradise to include beings that were all alike; His joy comes from knowing each of us including an understanding we can bring to Him that is unique, and therefore special. He made us look differently, and think differently, so that we could be unique, special, and accountable in life, and in passing.

The bond between the Father and His son exists now and forever within the cup of life that is the Holy Grail; if you prefer, you may call the cup of life the Holy Bond that every one of us drinks from. Fury claims it as the Holy Grail, and admits that the Father left it obvious enough to be discovered, and then in turn handed it back to humanity in understanding; God likes popular culture blended into His story, so the story takes on a popular sense of things.

All of mankind does drink freely and forever from the cup of life, knowing forgiveness and benefiting from salvation easily as the Father and son intended for every soul.

This story applies to all of humanity, and the success of the story matters. Readers represent success, and will lead to popularity. Increased popularity will deliver the results that the archangel will use in his earthly purpose. The archangel's earthly purpose will lead to heavenly happiness including great joy. True joy is hard enough to come by in life; heavenly joy is more common than earthly understanding of heavenly needs.

The son of God passed away on a cross of wood following mortal persecution and suffering, which was provided to him out of the free will of mankind. God watched and felt him suffer and embraced him upon his return. God accepted the outcome of that mission because he saw that the knowledge of forgiveness and eternal salvation had been received by mankind, and would be carried forward into progress.

Mortal forgiveness for life's trespass and our salvation in eternity is true and coming for all men, women and children for all time, thanks to the son of God, and to the Father's commitment to His son.

The son of God did journey on an earthbound mission to deliver the knowledge of eternal salvation of being and mortal forgiveness of sin and trespass for all of mankind. There is no requirement or license needed for you to gain eternal salvation and everlasting being. The son of God never maintained any requirement of commitment or any licensing agreement for you to attain his unconditional love. His original love for his father and his original love for man assured us forever of our place in God's heart, including our individual being within the Kingdom of Heaven. Being successful in eternity does necessitate equivalence; redemption through forgiveness following judgment is a bureaucratic eternal necessity, and the proper heavenly path to follow.

SECTION VII

Judgment and Equivalence
of Heavenly Beings

EVERY MORTAL BEING IN PASSING WILL REGAIN EQUIVALENCE IN heaven. The path to equivalence is through judgment day. When you die, and you will, you will become light. Your lighted soul will travel to the gates of heaven along with your life savings. Some of those life savings will be good, and some may be bad. You may have delivered goodness in life, and you may have delivered harm and sadness. You may have wronged someone so badly, that the wrong is maintained in their own life savings. They will carry that wrong with them to the gates of heaven and into the Kingdom of Light and may present the wrong back to you at your judgment day.

The higher order of eternal judgment is a necessary step so beings will function eternally without animosity. The purpose of judgment is simple, to re-establish lost equilibrium between beings. Can you imagine heaven existing with mortal animosity? Of course you can't. Heaven is heavenly, and it is perfection at the speed of light. The domain of earth is a domain that lacks equality of being; not by design, but perhaps out of necessity. There is no room for animosity when it comes to the heavenly speed of light.

Some of mankind is wealthy, and some of mankind struggles to feed itself; that is the ring of truth; some have too much, and some don't have enough. The rich and the poor live within the knowledge of the ring of truth, but may not know the importance contained within the balance of that truth. True power comes from knowledge only when the knowledge is put to use. The poor and hungry greatly outnumber the rich; that is truth today and hopefully not tomorrow.

Prevention of persecution and prevention of suffering are incumbent Godly pursuits placed upon mankind that are God's single modern commandment as provided in this gospel. This commandment does not come carved in ancient stone; this commandment comes carved with the ring of powerful truth through words that demonstrate the progressive nature of heavenly knowledge along with mortal understanding. Progress is reality; God's intent for His progressive future is apparent and part of your reality.

Judgment is a requirement, and will occur in the early stages of your return to heaven. Understanding that you are accountable to those you offended and hurt in life is important. Every being that you wronged during your mortal existence who maintains the wrong in their life savings can detain you through their own participation in your judgment day. The relevant thing is that their being is also retained with you at your judgment. There is no free ride when you seek justice; justice without cost does not make equality; if you desire justice, you must participate in the cost.

Heaven is compelling, and decisions do have to be made as to how much hurt you experienced in life, and the value of the hurt versus the value of going ahead to participate in the perfection of eternity's lighted world which is heaven.

For example, let's examine the case of a man who commits the mortal crime of murder. Let's imagine the man believes he is in love and that his love has been betrayed; he then murders his estranged wife in jealous rage, which is possible since man is flawed by nature. Along with the wife, the man cuts the throat of her youthful boyfriend. During that lifetime our murderer has now stopped two ongoing lives for which he will ultimately be forgiven. He will be forgiven thanks to God and the son, and the needs of the eternal world of heaven, and all beings. Every one of us is ultimately guaranteed immortal forgiveness for our earthly sin and trespass; you can count on that forgiveness as a forgone conclusion even though you may be made uncomfortable while you are facing the poor decisions you made during life.

During your mortal lifetime, you own the power of forgiveness. This power is part of your humanity. The power of human forgiveness is a great thing a human being possesses. This story is not the story of that human ability to provide forgiveness though. That forgiveness is yours to offer through the power of your consideration, your free will, and the great effort it sometimes takes to provide comfort.

Eternal forgiveness always follows judgment as part of the redemptive process; however, our murderous being that stopped two lives will have plenty to contend with at his judgment. He has wronged two beings directly. Each of those murdered beings may participate in judgment by remaining present with the murderer who took their life. Since the crime happened in time on earth, time spent waiting on personal forgiveness will become time served when the decision to move on is reached. Equivalence through judgment is a higher order objective, and critical. You cannot get into heaven without spending a little time acknowledging suffering; so, there is just a little pain, and much anticipation, in watching heaven go by without you.

It is understood that for many life is a struggle, and yet heaven is the compelling conclusion of life for everyone. You cannot get into heaven without finalizing the price of personal forgiveness when it is asked; alas, most judgment events are uneventful, and remain only a technical stepping stone into a heavenly existence.

Yes, forgiveness is yours and is coming, but personal cost has to be paid since equivalence is a necessity within eternity. Every being will eventually choose to move on into heaven, and reach the fun and pleasantness it affords. Dispensing with grievance quickly through forgiveness is not a bad decision, and is a quick way to attain heavenly equality. Some victims of murder are happy to arrive in heaven, even while knowing they passed away from life earlier than anticipated. Believe it, or not.

Any being can keep you occupied in judgment, as long as they remain present with you; then neither of you will enjoy heaven until redemption is reached, and forgiveness is offered and accepted. After the conclusion of judgment, your being is off to embrace heaven including a balance in understanding. The point of judgment and forgiveness is to erase animosity; so we must admit to animosity not in submission, but in admonition. Do not pretend it is cruel to face your attacker; you may avoid seeking justice if you do not bear the scars of cruelty; forgiving souls who turn the other cheek comfortably are not as uncommon as you would imagine; after all, life is a struggle, and fewer souls willingly carry those struggles with them through the gates of heaven.

The long grieving father, mother, brother, sister, friend, etcetera of our murder victims, along with every being who has interest that is reserved in their life savings, may participate in the judgment of our murderer. Indeed, many judgment day events are spectacular, and seating arrangements may be required. Sorry, even in heaven, front row seating remains at a premium. Seating arrangements are a puzzle not even heaven has figured out yet. God knows,

You may wonder why it is necessary to discuss Judgment Day at such length, and in such detail. Justice is a higher order process that delivers practical results, but requires eternal power, and coordinated effort to complete. Like all things that use such resources, planning leads to economically efficient results. An angel on earth has arrived to provide just a little guidance to the mortal world of man so a little preparation never hurts. It's God's plan to help you be prepared, and a little less fearful. Souls worrying about damnation in Hades don't really face the crisis of falling apart at the gates, but commotion and confusion can lead to distraction, and can confound progress. Just think about it, and you'll be fine. Death is real, and coming sooner or later, the gospel is intentionally designed to offer many things, including comfort.

Angels serve God and heavenly purpose as guides in order to help things down the road as mankind travels side by side with the Shepherd of humanity and heaven. Angels in heaven serve God the Shepherd, His heavenly bureaucracy, and all heavenly beings; angels on earth do the same thing.

Guidance that delivers knowledge is a good thing; not all the guidance and knowledge the simple messenger brings may appear so gentle and loving; not all things in God's universe can be gentle and loving alone; understanding and knowing God's goodness is one of life's great challenges.

Justice can be a hard thing to know, and to accept; God's justice may be the largest pill of all to swallow willingly; know that God carefully plans for His own justice; God's justice is the highest order, and at the top of your list of priorities to know; that medicine knowingly is delivered very carefully, so the least amount of true harm is delivered into living memory.

SECTION VIII

Love, Hate, and Redemption

ANGEL FURY DELIVERED THE FIRST OF THE MISSION'S STORIES IN 2015, and named it <u>The Gospel of Fury: The Gemini Star</u>. <u>The Gospel of Fury: The World of Make Believe</u> is the second story in the trilogy. The third story will be completed in 2017, and will be named <u>The Gospel of Fury: Redemption</u>.

Within <u>The Gospel of Fury: The Gemini Star</u>, Fury provides for admittance of God's First and Second Apocalypse marking man's forgiveness for early sin committed in the name of God, and any of His religions. Certain knowledge of apocalyptic events, and humanity's forgiveness for an epoch's worth of communal transgression against God would be enough single purpose for an angelic mission into the world of man, and his time on earth. <u>The Gemini Star</u> mission provides more purpose rather than limited purpose, since the tide now rises on the side of the angels and God, and the delivery of their own progressive knowledge.

Love God; fear God; praise God; appreciate God as He matches man's progress with progress of His own. Man's progress has increased exponentially; it stands to reason that God's progress must at least keep up with what He shepherds. The gospel delivers the Shepherd's progress now with an apparent exponential expanse of reason.

The first and second World Wars represent the first and second apocalyptic events. The Cold War, along with the assassination of President Jack Kennedy, marks the neutralization of the third apocalyptic event which was within sight of global destiny. Destiny, though, was averted by powerful eternal forces, and the onset of the third apocalyptic event was halted in its tracks. God provides His design through His simple star from creation to signal the event, and then provides His angelic messenger Fury, and gives our reasonable explanation.

Do not be caught too off guard or become offended; God did send His angel to explain calamity in God's name, and this written explanation delivers that judgment and forgiveness for all of humanity. The nature of the human condition, along with the history of mortal life, demonstrates that man understands personal loss gains attention through the pains of emotion; that destruction can provide deliverance when balance is restored by acknowledging the process of judgment, and that redemption is a good thing. This resulting explanation is gospel, and it is a good thing; not a thing intended to cause horror; but a thing to cleanse. The explanation completes the process; redemption, though, is a two way street, more or less.

Our own forgiveness was provided to us out of the Father's desire, and willingness, to accept His son's mission and message, in the way it was carried through history upon a cross of human flesh and bone and wood and nails. Our mass forgiveness requires the suffering of humanity on a larger scale, through the destruction provided by a world of warfare. These world wars are already written into the pages of fate, so the message of the gospel ties the known history into a knot of understanding. Don't shoot the messenger; don't waste time in sarcasm; be a good skeptic though.

Judgment without cost does not really provide equivalence; balance is not truly restored unless a price is established and paid. The adage "no pain, no gain," holds as true in heaven as it does on earth. The process of receiving redemption involves forgiveness through knowing, understanding, and acceptance. When God wants balance restored, there will be a price to pay. Receiving an invoice for a bill that is already paid should require no great leap of faith, even though it was a stiff tab.

That God chose to achieve the restoration of balance through His process of judgment and perceived punishment, rather than straight forward forgiveness, is God's concern, and your understanding to reason with. Messenger Fury's duty to God, and to man, was not to ignore the message, but to deliver the words fully, and with faith. God gives enough evidence to support the knowledge through His available stars that He tied to Fury's life, and this specific circumstance. God created the clarity first, then the compulsion to pass the message along to you, as sorrowful as that pearl of wisdom may be.

The deliverance of two apocalyptic events and the potential for the third is an important reminder to mankind that the lives we maintain, and the free will we exercise matter to God, and the Kingdom of Heaven. Love Him, praise Him, fear Him; He is God, the Supreme Being; try not to offend Him.

God is reaching into the world of today and tomorrow to remind us of our own significance, and to remind us of the importance of our actions and our decisions as a body of humanity. He is expanding our understanding of His view of us to not only include individual beings, but to include us as a body of beings; therefore He is increasing the level of accountability He sees in us.

This version of events is for all of humanity to know and understand. At times, man has been very bad during the more than two thousand years of recorded time since the son-of-God walked the earth. There is much historical evidence available to examine, to revisit, and to confront and admit; spiritual and religious atrocities throughout history contribute to the disgruntlement of the Supreme Being to the point that He is compelled to provide mass forgiveness for all of humankind. Attributing conflict and terror to heaven and God is not a good thing.

How can we really trust and admit that God sent the apocalyptic events? After all, He sent Fury into the world with the message you are reading now. The Archangel of the First Epoch provides the certainty of good truth with a clear explanation of forgiveness. The gospel will lay out plainly what God can provide as evidence based on what God can and did do through His powers of design together with His delivery through creation. He did send Fury; He did not send Happy; you can be happy knowing the truth of forgiveness.

These words of prophecy are yours to keep now, and any evidence you seek can be found within the life behind I. B. Fury, which can all be verified as reality. You can weigh the evidence God can provide through design and creation for what it is worth, and make your decision if the gospel you are reading is the gospel truth. You can also have a little faith; proof is only as good as what is available to present as evidence; stars and proof are mighty things when we see they come from God through design and creation to demonstrate intelligence. Adding up all the stars within the one life should provide enough of a balance to be convincing enough.

God first passed His Fury into the world of man long ago. Angel Fury is the father of the family of angels that study, learn, and maintain emotion. The lighted kingdom maintains things through practices and processes that don't exist naturally within light. Earth contains human nature naturally; heaven maintains human nature carefully; the reality of universal existence then remains in balance and understandable. God and heaven, and then, man and nature are the two sides to the reality of the mirrored universe of existence. Balance in understanding between these two realities requires His ingenuity to provide for, and to maintain. To help with the process of existence and understanding He enjoys assistance, and what makes Him happy creates joy in heaven, and on earth; angels serve Him gladly within His simple bureaucracy of administration, so that the balance of the mirrored reality serves heaven and earth.

Your expression of emotion maintains your humanity, so share your emotions wisely; enjoy the family of emotions fully; we angels are here but for another brief moment of time, and always available eternally. Of all the things you encounter in life it is your emotional well being, knowledge, and understanding that will have the most significant impact upon you and create the largest deposits into your life savings.

The Supreme Being cannot part the ocean for this gospel to demonstrate a miracle. He cannot shower the hungry with manna from heaven for The Gospel of Fury to show you that this is His good and modern word.

God will not break the rules of reality and science anymore than you yourself will break those rules during life. What He can and did do was deliver all the things He knows you want and need through the one life, and the company of angels that surround it. God chose to pass the being of angel Fury to the world for a special reason, to deliver this meaning filled message for these times.

Fury is one of the original emotions God discovered in creation when organic life was just a simple thing. The Supreme Being likes to watch as organic life develops and evolves. He admires those creations and revels in the changes of growth and adaptation. He never abandons hope for His own increasing levels of joy as things change and get better and better. When things get worse than before, just like every other being, He shrugs His shoulders and goes back to the drawing board; in His case, though, it is called His Rainbow of Creation.

One of the early things God noticed in creation was a thing He later called an emotion that originated when consumption of prey was just in its infancy. He witnessed an act of predation that lead to increasing levels of excitement and aggression within an organism while it attacked and consumed its victim. The results appeared to represent a higher degree of success including efficiency during the predatory consumption of organic life. He named that early emotional energy fury, and then, right away, created a being to watch over it, and named the being Fury to keep things easy to understand. He used the expression angel, because the being was going to pass messages concerning the thing to God. Angel means messenger in heaven, as it does on earth.

Emotions like love and hate came into existence much later as life evolved. All along the path of creation God has matched beings to His creations so He could keep things organized. His is a complex universe, and keeping organization simple helps with His divinely inspired administration.

Angel Love and Angel Hate are currently living daughters of the family of emotion angels. Emotion angels are abundant in heaven since being human means being emotional, and since humans have to maintain their humanity, heaven has to be able to assist human being. We are created in the image of our emotional God, and so heaven has to support humanity as God intended humanity to exist. God is extremely emotional; surprisingly, many more humans are extremely emotional than those that are less emotional.

Ancient angel Fury was entrusted by God to go into the world to watch and learn; then to be compelled at the right moment in time to deliver God's word during the changing of the epoch, to admit man must grow out of his childhood into his adulthood.

The circumstances of His desire along with His design and creation are laid out in the original story The Gospel of Fury: The Gemini Star.

God's message is plain and simple. These paths are the paths that He can use to clearly show His intent and His intelligence. Studying the truth in these stories, along with the facts of the mortal lives they represent, is worthwhile. The facts of creation tie our existence together with God when you accept that creation is not simply an accident, but a divinely inspired act designed to create coincidence, and to establish a pattern of truth to celebrate God, heaven, and man.

Pray for mankind not to waste our time; pray for mankind not to let this moment become one of historical reflection only. This is our opportunity to create legacy; this is your moment to embrace that opportunity; shape existence into what you would imagine existence should look like; witness His clear intent and purpose; act and embrace this moment for His greatest glory.

SECTION IX

Not Just Any Star:
The Greatest Star of All Time

ON FRIDAY, JUNE 3RD, 2016, DURING THE TIME WHEN THIS STORY was being written, the Greatest of all Time turned his eternal being to God and said, "Good Lord, is it my time now?"

Muhammad Ali, the Greatest of all Time, quipped further with God, "Now are we ready, Great God? For just this one more time, will it be my time to shine? Just as special in life, and especially in passing, do I yet remain the Greatest of all Time, Great God?"

The Lord then looked back to Cassias Clay Muhammad Ali and said, "Yes, Greatest, we are ready, and it is time. Yes, you are the Greatest of all Time; so yes, go on, and shine brightly for the entire world to see one more time and then forever more."

Muhammad Ali replied to the Lord, "I am coming to the gates of heaven now, Lord. Open the gates up wide Lord; a big man is coming through. Today, I will land softly just like a butterfly, but sting deeply just like a bee, just for your story, great Lord in heaven; my brilliant star for all to see shining brightly one more time, just for me to be here with you, Lord, here and now, and forever more."

God replied casually to His friend, "I know, I know; just remember the time difference, Greatest. We won't be opening the gates just yet. You mortal beings, now suddenly existing in light alone, take a fair amount of time to travel from the earth back to eternity. So take your time, ride the light, and enjoy your passing."

God's stars are for caring and sharing. So the finder of stars gathers Muhammad Ali's star of passing, to add to the growing bag of evidence provided by God to demonstrate intent, purpose, and intelligence. The Archangel of the First Epoch, angel Fury, Star Finder and Presenter of Keys, was born on June 3rd 1963, while Cassias Clay Muhammad Ali passed away on June 3rd, 2016. My date of birth June 3, and his date of death June 3, coincident to one another, is a miracle the designer and creator of the modern mission can provide for all man to see this story is gospel and necessary.

It is easy to find stars when you know where to look; presenting the keys to you helps you to see His mystery, and to know Him more simply.

This star of passing is not any common star, nor is it any common coincidence; this is the "Greatest" star of passing, and the "Greatest" common coincidence God and eternity could provide for His modern story. Muhammad Ali passed away on Fury's birthday June 3rd, also the day the Pope died in 1963, the day Fury was born. This star of coincidence exists so that I. B. Fury can write the Gospel of Fury as ongoing prophecy. Current events in the world created through God's design and creation develop and shape the gospel into real time prophecy so the world can witness clearly the reality and purpose of God.

This is a purpose-filled world, and this prophecy is purposeful.

What more would you like for your story? What more do you need to see? How easy can it be for you to simply ask me? There is only so much time, so ask freely, and we shall see if God can give you exactly what you need from His prophecy.

SECTION X

God's Apocalyptic Hammers of Justice

THE ARCHANGEL OF THE FIRST EPOCH OF MANKIND ADMITS GOD'S intelligence through His design and creation, so that the representation is reasonably sound, and creates relevance to the circumstances within our reality of life and time, so that events as titanic as mankind's apocalyptic judgment and forgiveness can be seen as having been driven into the world of mankind by the Supreme Being out of intent and purposefully.

Praise Him, love Him, and fear Him. Accept the little things He can provide as stars and accept the keys to see them as His great miracles in order to welcome Him, and make Him feel at home. He is the shepherd, and is planning for the future we cannot see.

Mankind will probably not simply accept that a true act of God has occurred without evidence, so without evidence there could be no reasonable claim for the miracle of forgiveness, or that an act of God has occurred. Humanity's complete forgiveness for the numerous transgressions of destruction committed during childhood is described now in this text. The available evidence applied as proof of God's forgiveness is supplied through stars of coincidence that pass through the angel's life that are identified and provided as keys by Fury.

That God assures the forgiveness through <u>The Gospel of Fury</u> could be taken on plain faith, but plain faith alone in a story of words will not conclude in permanent understanding and knowledge of the world of reality.

God did lay the plainness of apocalyptic truth into the world, leaving the icing on the cake to be applied by the paltry messenger claiming to be Archangel Fury. If it were not so unlikely, then it would seem reasonable, though possibly not probable. Yet here is God's forgiveness of humanity (following the age of his childhood) for you to accept.

A miracle may remain small in nature. That it comes from God through design and creation, and shows His intelligence, makes the miracle. If God's work can be seen plainly enough, then celebrate it simply enough through acceptance.

The Gospel of Fury contains the truth and the reality of facts that pass through Fury's life in support of the gospel. The Supreme Being's design and creation passing through the crossroad of one life may be enough to convince some skeptics, and that is all God was asking for at the beginning of The Gemini Star. He only asked for a reduction in the level of doubt; not the elimination of doubt.

At the beginning of The Gemini Star, God did not ask for complete belief. God only asked for fewer oblivious souls arriving at the gates of heaven. He did not say He required the total belief of all of humanity. He does not ask for total belief and faith or knowing. He only asks for an open heart, and a chance to explore innocence.

Every simple and straightforward path of worship and belief is a fine path to God and heaven. Every soul belongs, and is welcome at the gates of heaven, including the oblivious souls who fall apart from the sudden but overwhelming joy in fully knowing universal goodness.

How can we know that World War I represents the shepherd's display of His generational power over humanity through His creativity in design and His delivery of intelligence through the creation of human life? We can look backwards into history and see that popular belief already describes the world wars as apocalyptic events. Archangel Fury, as verifier of the Apocalypse, is here to put the seal on the deal.

The hammer of World War I is God's first apocalyptic strike, but only His beginning blow to deliver apocalyptic justice. Apocalyptic justice serves His purpose by restoring His sense of comfort and balance between heaven and earth. He does not rest well knowing abuse in His name survives without repentance. Our knowledge of His apocalyptic justice restores His comfort, and balance is delivered, and then judgment is complete.

Love the Lord, praise the Lord, fear the Lord; no longer abuse the Lord in name.

Fight your own wars against each other all day and all night; do not fight religious wars, and do not kill each other over religion or commit terror. These are His rules as you enter into the second epoch of man.

The one and only Queen Mother Victoria of the United Kingdom gives rise to progeny who will become the crown heads of Europe at the start of World War I. God's angel on earth, Queen Victoria, and her family of messengers, rule Europe's countries at the start of the First World War. Whether you want to know that the Queen Mother and her family existed as angels on earth is for you to decide. That God sends messengers called angels is self evident. Archangel Fury, who is head of his earthly mission, tells you this is gospel and that the royal characters and facts of their lives are evidence now. God ties their historic reality directly into Fury's angelic life through His design and creation to piece it together as His miracle in a straight forward manner so that you can accept it on more than just hope and faith. Although hope and faith are worthy, we want to deliver a little more than just testimony. Man the skeptic is an adult now, and stories alone may no longer help him sleep soundly at night.

Enjoy your rest, mankind; the shepherd is here to watch over your future with Him.

Three or four heavenly days ago, a generation of angels was delivered by God into a family to signal the onset of the delivery of balance between humanity and heaven. You could use your internet search engine right now and Wikipedia to view and research the characters of Queen Victoria's children and grand children. You may notice and agree in sympathy that they are angelic in appearance, character, and may be odd or unworldly in their manner. I doubt they knew they were harbingers of the beginning of an apocalypse. Then again, the royal family helped to thrust the world into war.

It is God's generational power over humanity that enables one family group of mortal beings to find their paths into positions of governance over an entire continent for the purpose of His historic theater. He maintains generational power over humanity through creation; this is an important thing to accept, so believe it, or not. Doubting God's greatness, and doubting His abilities, though, would not be the best demonstration of our own wisdom. He lays His plan out plainly enough for you to see; we can only watch and see if I. B. Fury writes the story well enough for you to help popularize it just as God intends for it to be popularized. His legacy lies in the balance, and time is fleeting.

How and why would God send angel's to the earth to tell all concerning the delivery of the apocalyptic event designed to restore balance between God and man? Other than angels, what would He send to signal such a significant event? Humankind's en masse forgiveness for sin and trespass in His name is important, and does matter to heaven and earth. It is not up to angel Fury to ignore God's vision and stars; it is only up to Fury to admit the plain truth.

He does send His messengers once in a special while; He did leave a visible history for the knowing messenger to find; He is benevolent and intends for us to benefit from the knowledge. There is deliverance in knowing, so He had to send a knowing being into time, and into life to help you see; your role is only to know.

God's furious thunder and lightening, while impressive and terrifying, cannot tell a story; angels are sent for that. The anger in earthquakes and the fury of tornados may foster attention; yet they cannot point to His words. Angel Anger and angel Fury, however intimidating they may sound, can only tell a simple tale, and hope you understand the need to be redeemed.

That He sent the brothers angel Fury and angel Anger into the world on a mission together is telling enough to understand His need for satisfaction. It was never a good idea to make war and commit slaughter in the name of God, the son-of-God, nor any of His spirit or religion. Do you not imagine He would need to seek retribution? Do you not imagine He would allow you to grow into adulthood and understanding, then send powerful things to make you know Him closer, to know He can suffer from emotional pain? Or, did you anticipate He would turn the other cheek, and allow you to enter the next two thousand years fighting and warring over spirituality? Argue and talk about God and your belief all you like, just play nicely and remain polite.

The apocalyptic events are well enough in the past now so that little of the sorrow still survives. The epoch has turned, and this is the time for the telling of God's story. Your task is simple; take up the story, spread the gospel into the world of today, and hope for the delivery of the promise.

Time is fleeting for all mortal beings, and angels are no exception; angels on earth may be just a little more anxious to leave all too quickly, too. We will take our own desire for the promise with us. The quest is at hand with all hope for success lying within each of you.

Forgiveness is yours, so you may accept it and the meaning God intends. Equivalence through judgment and the redemption it enables, will achieve balance between heaven and earth, as long as it is shared and known.

How do we know for sure God intended two apocalyptic events? The double apocalyptic events are self evident since we are left with the visible history of World War I and World War II.

Why does God bring the knowledge of two and potentially three apocalyptic events then bind them together, yet also keep them separate and distinct? So that we understand the severity of His distress with us, and know that His displeasure rose to the level for decisive action and the distinctive deliverance of two clear apocalyptic events, while threatening a third.

God's apocalyptic hammer of justice struck once, then it struck a second time; it was scheduled to strike a third time. God was just not sure of His feelings; feelings are real to every being, even the Supreme Being. After all, what good would there be in being the Supreme Being without feelings and emotions? Because of His indecision, God defaulted to the Covenant that He maintains with mankind, and then called off the third apocalyptic event.

The universal Covenant you can welcome and accept on faith. God's cancellation of the third apocalyptic event demonstrates and supports the Covenant that states that mankind is good enough. You will witness the Covenant in action now, and in the future, as you move forward in progress with God.

Fury himself is bound by the Covenant, and must not deny mankind anything based on his desires, perceptions, or fears. Our spiritual future is yours to shape; God will steer spiritual destiny as it approaches; make sure the book of fate records our spiritual story as you intend for it to read; spiritual do-over's are hard to come, by since spiritual cake is cooked in heaven. Eat wisely while you can eat at all.

Fury delivers the Covenant, and then has added another theme to the list of themes pouring out of The Gospel of Fury. The collection of coincidence and themes within the single life of Fury, and his family of angels on earth, demonstrates God's modern benevolence, together with His intelligent support of these gospels. In other words, the proof lies within the pudding.

You can understand and maintain the knowledge of the Covenant, that we all are good enough, and that is all. To be good enough as a collection of human beings is good enough; to be good enough in the eyes of the Lord, the shepherd of humanity is enough; it is also a great and fortunate thing. Play however you choose as men, but use care when you play with His name. There is more power and control available to Him through generational design and creation than living souls can know. Love Him, praise Him, and fear Him; to fear God is a wise and good thing, and a common practice in the Kingdom of Light.

Generational nationalism existing prior to the onset of World War II developed following the end of World War I. Historians have provided testimony and evidence regarding the conditions that lead to decades of warfare at the turn of the twentieth century. The naming of the two wars we discuss as World War I and World War II binds them together uniquely into man's history. The Cold War stayed cold, thank God.

Advances in technology along with changing styles of government in the world following World War I and World War II lead to military proliferation, and perceived conflicts of interest that enabled the onset of the Cold War. The posturing of China and Russia against Europe and the United States was creating a path to what would have amounted to catastrophic warfare.

The potential for World War III is in evidence now. Historians can verify that for you better than Fury can, but it is not idol gossip to remind you that nuclear weapons were maintained on alert at alarming levels of expediency. This spiritual story is not designed to explain the detailed history that lead to the mud slinging trench warfare of WWI, followed by the genocidal rage of WWII, and the impending threat of nuclear war which would have been known as WWIII. This spiritual explanation is important but simple, and is designed to facilitate humanities opportunity to know redemption on a global scale at the changing of the heavenly epoch. One heavenly month has passed now since the child God embraces walked the earth.

God the creator delivered His star of confirmation through Fury's own daughter who was born into the world by design and creation on January

22, 2001. That is exactly one hundred years after Queen Victoria passes back to heaven on January 22, 1901. That star from creation may not completely wow you, but that is what God can provide to us to help unlock mystery with the key presented by messenger Fury. You can choose to understand and accept humanity's forgiveness from God, as described here for the first two thousand years of mans transgression and sin for wrongful acts committed in the name of God and His religion. A single mystery should just require one key to unlock. There are many keys He gives in the Gospel of Fury. Collect all the keys in the story so you can share the truth of the gospel, and deliver the popularity Fury asks for. Spread the gospel; if not for Fury; for humanity; and for heaven's sake.

The price of judgment and forgiveness has already been paid. The global warfare is part of history now, and fading into the past, and the pain is felt less today. The coincidence of a date of death January 22, 1901, and a date of birth January 22, 2001, and the timing of exactly one century is what He can share with us through His design and creation, and the telling of this story.

Through The Gospel of Fury: The Gemini Star, angel Fury delivers God's Covenant that He maintains with man. Restated simply, and taken on faith, the covenant is that "man is good enough". That is simple, and that is all.

How do we know that God, our Supreme Being in heaven, really reached out and cancelled such a thing as a third apocalyptic strike of His hammer of justice? We had the Cold War well under way, and we know that the nuclear weapons were at the ready. There were some close calls that could have lead to nuclear obliteration. One hot head too many and watch out; do over for humanity. World War III would have kept the watch angels busy at the gateway to heaven. (The gateway is just to keep beings organized by the way, don't worry; you'll get in one way or the other.)

History shows us that the apocalyptic wars were all related to one another, and that they grew from one another is a matter of record.

Together they represent our apocalyptic history that we share with heaven and the Supreme Being. The fact that the Cold War never developed into World War III, means that it was called off by God; if you are a believer in apocalyptic history, and God, that is. The Cold War was waiting in destiny's path, scheduled to arrive on time as planned. The arms of war had been invented, manufactured, deployed, and were there at the ready. The national powers were aligned against one another, and everyone was watching for the right or wrong moment to unleash madness. Love Him, Praise Him; above all fear his generational power over humanity. Your well being depends on understanding Him simply.

God recognized the Covenant that man is good enough so the massive destruction of the third apocalyptic event was not visited on the earth and humanity. The cancellation of the third apocalyptic event is a good thing. Apocalyptic events are like earthquakes; each level of destruction is ten times that of its predecessor. So World War II was ten times as devastating as World War I, and World War III would have been ten times as destructive as World War II. That would indicate that World War III would have been a thousand times as bad as World War I. Be thankful for His mercy, and understand that we are good enough, and that is enough in itself.

The cancellation of the third apocalyptic event is marked with a star, and the key presented by Fury, but made available originally through His design and creation using a birthday, and tied into the gospel you are reading for history. The stars that are presented in the gospel are each a matter of historical record, and will be verified later by researchers, and then conclusions can be presented by authors who can write better than an angel can.

The assassination of the American President John Kennedy on November 22, 1963 is a key to unlock mystery. Fury had arrived on earth by then, and Pope Saint John XXIII had passed away, both events occurring coincidentally on June 3, 1963.

Yes, it is an unhappy thought to imagine God would use unpleasant events like war and assassination to demonstrate and explain His version of reality, but God does work in mysterious ways. He has to use the things He has available to demonstrate the certainty of His reality for His skeptical human beings. You only have to keep watching for His stars and accept the stars as the keys to the kingdom.

God, the Supreme Being, ties the Presidential assassination star of 1963 to His messenger angel Redemption. He chooses not just any named angel; He chooses angel Redemption, who is forgiveness. This was God's choice of the place to pin His star, and to provide your key to His mystery.

Be conscious that the truths of these gospels are not Fury's creations for a story, and that the acts do not belong to Fury. Fury is an honest messenger passing gospel truth from heaven to earth. These acts of God signal the cycle of humanity's redemption, and that the moment of understood forgiveness is at hand. That the moment falls onto the turn of the first epoch into the second epoch is just a matter of God's perfect timing.

Angel Redemption was born May 29, 1968 by an act of creation which He uses to display His abilities and purposefulness. The form of a birthday coincidence is provided so you recognize heavenly truth. John Kennedy was born May 29, 1917. The coincidence of the birth days of John Kennedy and angel Redemption is what God can show us so we may see His ability through the fog of mystery.

The archangel presents as chief of the mission, similar to the queen bee of the bee hive surrounded by her worker bees. The archangel serves the purpose God lays before the being. God gives the being of the archangel the strengths and weaknesses necessary to insure His intents and purpose are reached. Archangel Fury possesses the ability to see the superpowers of the angels that surround him and belong to God's mission. The mission in this case is The Gemini Star.

It was early in 2014 that God compelled angel Fury to tell his spouse that she was the angel Redemption. This followed a family argument during which Redemption displayed character traits unfamiliar to Fury. The event caused a night of fitful sleep, and provided an unrelenting compulsion to admit to a truth that had not previously occurred to Fury. So, Fury woke up the next day and dutifully proclaimed to his wife that she was an angel on earth, and specifically the angel of redemption who is forgiveness. She took the news well, but it took a while to sink in. I guess when you tell your wife she's an angel, it's a good thing; but, when you tell her she is the angel Redemption, it just makes her wonder what that may entail. She did not even appear to take the news with a grain of salt; she only appeared to accept the idea, and consider it carefully. Her experience with spirituality and God is based on her own relationship to eternal being, and those things she talks to God and the son about, and not for me to speculate over in public.

As 2014 progressed, the identities of Fury's family of twelve angels became apparent, at least in Fury's imaginative mind anyway. We can admit that if God were sending a mission to earth, He would design His humans carefully so that the message would not be lost. Any failed mission would be a waste of time and resources. Man maintains free will; God's evidence of Himself has to be conclusive, or humans won't step in front of the firing line of skepticism and sarcasm in any attempt to write a modern gospel.

Gradually and over time, the character of angelic being living on earth has become obvious; angels are practical things and lead a practical existence. Time has passed and one by one, Fury has attempted to alert his family members that they were angels on earth. Giving them each a heads up, however minimal it may have been, clears the path for this story to unfold into the light of criticism.

The 2014 year of lightening culminated during the Christmas season when God compelled angel Fury to admit to angel Love directly that she was an angel on earth, and had suffered through a life of learning about all things having to do with her own superpower love. Like her sister she took the news in a friendly enough manner. I guess when you tell someone they are an angel; it is not actually a bad piece of news, plus she maintains a kind heart for her rather intense cousin.

2014 was the year angel Fury became lightened, and discovered the nature of his family of angels on earth. God's mission filled with intent and purpose would unfold the following year 2015, and develop into The Gospel of Fury: The Gemini Star.

The angel Redemption had been named long before God showed Archangel Fury the evidence of the apocalyptic events of the twentieth century. The good Lord is generous, and provides knowledge for those who wish to see. (I. B. Fury has spent a lifetime studying God's message. When I was nineteen years old, I sent a letter to the Christian Broadcasting Network, alerting them that I was the anti-Christ. They wrote back and acknowledged that, "everyone should follow the path God lays out for them.")

It was after angel Redemption was named that God delivered the star of Jack Kennedy's May 29 birthday, which matches Redemption's birthday of May 29. This simple birthday star from creation provides a valuable key of knowledge which can increase our understanding of a real heavenly action, which was our release from the grip of the third apocalyptic event. This news is probably hard to believe. That heaven could actually reach into the world with this level of detail should create wonder, skepticism, and possibly alarm; then again the world should have anticipated a level of detail that would dissuade us from skepticism, deliver certainty, and calm fears that God would ignore humanity at this point in history.

You have been waiting for the second coming at just the right time; you can have a messenger instead of the son; you can determine if the gospel provides enough, or whether we should ask God for more.

As was mentioned earlier, God hopped off the fence of indecision, and stopped the disastrous event since mankind is good enough to be simply forgiven whenever God faces indecision. That man is good enough is His Covenant. God's sense of balance was restored following two apocalyptic strikes, which is horror enough for any world.

Jack's father Joseph Kennedy Sr. had long planned for a Kennedy to occupy the White House. Jack Kennedy's older brother was destined to fill that role. Alas, he had the wrong birthday, and the gospel and truth matter more than a single life. Jack's older brother Joe Kennedy born July 25, 1915, died in combat August 12, 1944. His earthly remains were never recovered.

Jack Kennedy, the future president of the United States, upon learning the news that his brother had been killed in combat, uttered the phrase, "So, now it falls to me." Jack became the thirty-fifth president, and subsequently took an unlikely bullet to the back of his head on November 22, 1963. For all you conspiracy theorists, here you have the Lord's truth. John F. Kennedy served the Lord directly, and his assassination is a tragic star signaling the end of God's apocalyptic cycle of justice.

Look into Jack's eyes and you will see his soul, and you will know the truth; he always knew he was doomed. God's presence was with him throughout his life, every step of the way to that 1963 day of destiny in Dallas, Texas when he was assassinated while travelling in an open convertible. His fate was written long ago, probably before the angel was even born. His star from May 29, 1915 to November 22, 1963 represents part of a key to understanding mankind's redemption, and the conclusion of the Supreme Beings apocalyptic cycle. It is intentionally presented to you at the changing of the epoch to show you God's power and intelligence, while providing the knowledge of deliverance. Bringing all these modern things you need in one set of gospel stories, enabled by a family of angels on earth, delivered by God, sounds like a fairly straight forward approach into our reality.

Jack Kennedy was an angel of God, and doomed to serve His purpose. It is no small purpose, though; this turning of the first epoch into the second epoch is an important time for the world. Our purpose now is to acknowledge heaven, and to recognize global man, and to bring these closer together into understanding. Humanity's forgiveness for committing slaughter and war in God's name is a reality you can live with. The universe is vast and filled with many worlds, each world having certain stages the shepherd plans and provides for.

The world's apocalyptic events ensure the future of humanity rolls out according to the shepherd's long ranging plans. Believe it; the second epoch will roll into the third epoch in two-thousand years. The Gospel of Fury provides God's words here so that the future of the earth, and of humanity, moves toward Him, not away from Him. Commit your crimes and have your wars, but never commit crime in His name, and never again commit war and slaughter in His name. Those abuses in His name were the result of mankind's childhood; move with Him now into adulthood, and move closer to Him united in progress.

SECTION XI

Angelic Lightening

ANGELIC LIGHTENING TAKES PLACE WHEN GOD'S MESSENGER(S) ON earth awaken to their understanding of the existence of the full truth and power of eternal being, and begin to gain knowledge of heaven's essential intent and purpose. Essential intent and purpose being delivered by heaven would indicate naturally, or unnaturally, that the message cannot be ignored. Understanding and knowledge gained through the messenger's lightening then becomes a mortal burden that cannot be denied. To deny heavenly intent and purpose would expose all of humanity to the potential of missing out on God's message, when it may have been very carefully crafted by the Supreme Being, and no one would want that to be ignored or missed.

An angels lightening may never be fully complete, and does not occur in a single breath, or one single stroke of inspiration. God's special messengers are so rare that it takes great amounts of coincident circumstance to convince the mortal messenger of heaven's intent, and to present enough circumspect evidence to describe heaven's purpose, including the story God wants to tell.

Most people would say that even hoping to meet a lightened angel on earth, let alone become one, is a fool's errand; if the errand is God's errand, the errand is not foolhardy.

Love God, praise God, fear God; do not treat God foolishly.

Responsibility for the messenger's self awareness is the heavenly portion of the development of angelic lightening; man's acceptance of the messenger's angelic being on earth is the mortal world's responsibility and choice. A fully lightened angel has had its burden lightened from itself when man openly shares the burden God has placed on mortal existence. Lightening the angel's burden is a good thing.

Angelic burden is lifted and the angel rises when the purpose of the mission's message is known and shared between heaven and earth. A fully lightened angel brings heaven and earth closer together through the understanding that the message was indeed heavenly sent and is accepted in knowing God has time today to share truth with man; that is a big step for mankind.

Togetherness between heaven and man will exist even when only a degree of truth is at least examined across spiritual and religious groups, by the wisdom of experts. Even just the attempt to understand and to question will remove enough of global doubt to ease God's concern over the number of oblivious souls arriving at heaven's gates.

Equality, happiness, and togetherness between heaven and earth benefits immortal and mortal being, since God will spread His joy between the two realities He enjoys. There is enough reality already in The Gospel of Fury to answer questions over whether or not God cared enough to send His choice of modern words into the world. All you really need to do is consider whether or not The World of Make Believe helps you to believe just a little bit more modernly, and decide whether to spread the word or not. As long as you keep the personal door to your heart open enough; God will put His foot into the space you provide. The world's acceptance of liberty of belief, and the freedom to explore possibility between one another, will continue progress and carry the future, and the Shepherd will take care of the rest.

Heaven's joy may be a little harder to recognize. Keep in mind there is a distinction between time in heaven and earth. It takes a serious moment to make the earth a happier place; heaven on earth is worth waiting for though. When the light of heaven does shine, the earth shines along with it. Be patient and scrutinize these words in line with the facts.

The gospel truth of the matter is that earth and man provide things heaven needs; heaven provides eternal hope for the world and other things man needs. Heaven needs things man can provide just as much as man hopes to find heaven. Hopefully you will discover heaven on earth when enough of this gospel is weighed, and the truth of the words is discovered and the gospel is shared. A trending gospel is a happy gospel; a viral gospel may be too much to hope for.

An angel on earth can only be as effective as His design and creation enables the resulting life to demonstrate. It is God's eternal power passing into man's earthly reality that must demonstrate enough things man needs, so that man sees God's intent and purpose clearly enough to foster growing knowing, and lasting impression.

Belief, faith, and knowing are differing levels of spiritual understanding. Modern man has reached a developed stage of human progress now. Mankind can witness a demonstration of God's power through design and creation intelligently, and challenge the facts of existence as they are placed into the reality of life through these stories. In other words, if it reads like the word of God, delivers purpose like the word of God would, and is backed up by the reality of the life of the archangel who is at the center of the word, then it must be the word of God. He likes to send it, so believe in His magic.

Lightening the Archangel's burden through popularity frees angel Fury to deliver what he knows as heaven's great wish for the epoch. Heaven's great wish for the passage of the epoch is for man to demonstrate trust and faith in the earthbound Archangel of the First Epoch, and to live in worldwide trust and faith for this moment of time so the Father in heaven can deliver, and then receive, His earthly legacy.

The Father in heaven can further demonstrate His desire for any grandchild of the epoch. Knowingly, or not knowingly, the entire world must ask if there is enough love to support any grandchild admitted to be of Him in being. This world can be a harsh place, filled with difference of opinion that can be astonishing; for a believer there is hope; for a cynic there is no hope; for a healthy skeptic there is much possibility.

The Archangel of the First Epoch knows what to do with the popularity afforded by the gospel stories; Fury needs the tools to complete the great quest of our time. Just the passion of dreaming and hoping for the possibility of a child born of prophecy may be enough in and of itself for this epoch; the reality of a child is an obligation only God can plan and provide for.

The main mission entrusted to the messenger of the epoch is complete in the delivery and preservation of the modern message; Fury and the mission angels shall go back to God and heaven, with or without the legacy provided by the earthborn child of heritage, depending on the real time result of The Gospel of Fury. The preservation of the words of the gospel truth delivers man's future as the Supreme Being intends; in that alone there is success, and heaven's happiness is assured.

It may not be the people of the age of the epoch who accept and guide modern belief and knowing, which is fine. You don't always get everything you want when you want; but you get what you need by design. Much like prophecy, man's wisdom is clearer when mankind can look backwards.

The horizon of destiny is not yet close enough to be clear, so the book of fate is thus still being written in 2016. Success for Fury at the passing of the epoch, through a worldwide demonstration of faith in God's love of diversity within spiritual practice, while establishing faith in the purpose of unity toward God, and Fury's desire for heaven's legacy, remains up to the people of the epoch to consider.

Have faith the child of God walked the earth two-thousand years ago; believe the child walked the earth so heaven and earth, exist together more closely; know God will keep creating the things that He wants, during the epoch and beyond. Know that the child of the epoch will not come into poverty. Have faith that the Father demonstrated His desire to deliver the spirit of the child; have faith that the Archangel can deliver the child; know that there is a covenant maintained with God that man is good enough. He does not ask for more until He has what He needs.

The Gemini Star demonstrates the lightening of angel Fury in order to deliver essential being with firm understanding, into the world of modern man. The World of Make Believe represents the rise of the angel on earth as it approaches powerful mankind with truth, and the hope of delivering heaven into the modern world of knowledge, to promote understanding and acceptance in the modern messages.

Man and his skepticism exist hand in hand; noble angels and God, the Father of creation, embrace one another fully. A fully lightened archangel on earth existing to celebrate the turning of the first epoch into the second epoch is truth, and satisfies God's initial desire; searching for heavenly stars and dreaming of delivering God's legacy into being is a wish and hope for man's worldwide progress toward unity of understanding, and simple agreement in spirituality may be too much to ask for.

There are important things representing God in this testimony; God sends important things very rarely. These things He sends are simply stated, but are described with some mystery in some cases, and leave a little ambiguity, since some of the things are fantastical. These things are your responsibility. Responsibility and accountability are real for adults; study this gospel thoroughly so that you make thoughtful decisions. Indecision and inaction yield results, as do decisive action.

This is God's plan, sent through His design, which has been illustrated through acts of creation that demonstrate His capability and intelligence. Embracing His modern word as it is delivered through this story, and maintaining faith while the real time prophetic reality of the world unfolds is a rare opportunity which creates a challenge for those who desire to witness the potential results that popularity and success can provide. This modern story is your story to finish.

What God wants is a little less doubt and confusion in the world, along with a future for mankind that keeps God's heavenly goodness, and leaves man responsible and accountable; everything else The Gospel of Fury provides is gravy; gravy does add flavor, though, and the world needs the flavor of the epoch to prepare the path to the future as the Shepherd intends.

SECTION XII

Angel Hate the Thirteenth Angel

GOD GAVE MANY THINGS FOR HIS EPOCH MISSION TO EARTH. MANY of these things can been described to you in words, and there is evidence provided to you by using facts to show coincidence. You can refer to these things as coincident fact that fits the purpose, or you can elevate the things into miracles. The things God gives to the mission enable Him to achieve His goals, and in some cases demonstrate intent, and to leave the world with the impression He intends. If you see the things He provides clearly as intent, it helps the story become worthy of something as great as a gospel for the epoch.

Fury's personal gifts are given by God through creation and by design to serve intent and purpose. This is some of God's magic, and has to do with the power and presence of eternal being which includes mortal insight, intelligence, and intuition. Those personal God given gifts are complicated tools, and to share them with you is not as easy as telling you the coincident nature of a birth date, and labeling angel Fury anti-Christ since he was born 6/3/63, the same day the Pope died. I accept the miracle of coincidence whenever I see it in the presence of eternal purpose. The personal gifts are tools given by God to insure the mission's success, and that the things God sends are interpreted as close to what God means as is humanly possible.

Father in heaven has no desire to send a mission to earth that will fail. Father in heaven has no desire to send an angel that will just consider delivering the gospel for the modern age. Father in heaven can use His power over humanity to ensure His design and creation is as fool proof as necessary, from inception to conclusion. It has been said that God is more artist than architect since man does maintain free will. All of time exists within the universe of eternity; so, in theory as we understand it, God knows outcomes, but lives with some results that may be less than desirable. I know He was not thrilled that the son-of-God was pinned to a cross while delivering forgiveness and salvation; but it seems mankind has survived the first epoch, and that Christianity as we know it serves God's purpose.

He can change the world by creating a generation of beings who will deliver what He wants to shape the world, and He can send a family of messengers to carry out His special needs. He can shape the path of the world He shepherds; He can bring one life along the path He intends from its birth to its destiny.

Some lives are lived within an eternal presence that brings our eternal being into clearer focus, possibly at a subconscious level that we can clearly admire later by examining the path of our lives when what appeared to be the faint trail of life becomes the paved road we seemed to have freely created and followed; possibly that faint trail later appears to have been a divided four lane highway designed to get us to where the great power intentionally drove us. The great power of eternity is individual being; the great director of course always remains God. Intent that serves a great purpose uses eternal individual being one step at a time, to guide us all along a path that may serve a function that we cannot yet fully understand yet someday may. Billions and billions of beings support a mirrored universe of existence, designed intelligently so that life makes sense that God can enjoy on a personal level. Stars and rocks are not the greatest company, and not a higher order of existence; life is the highest order, intelligent life relating one being to another being, and is the highest possible achievement within the universe God created. Admitting God cares for us completes the circle of existence. Rocks are just rocks; without intelligent beings there is no purpose for the universe; God created the universe to provide a space for being including purpose, which includes everlasting being and essential continuity.

Mankind maintains free will, and not everything goes perfectly according to the artist's design, but creation has a way of delivering each of us to our relevant fate. Genetics are a heavenly tool needing generations to carefully craft, when clear objectives require special lives to deliver heavenly goals. The power of our spiritual being does make a difference in our mortal lives and helps us along the path we are more or less willing to create and follow. Your eternal being may have more influence over yourself than another person's eternal being has in their life. Indeed, there are those of us that are a little more touched than others. Intuition is closely related to the idea of being touched. I live now as a human being, and cannot claim to understand the rules of eternal being, and why some people are extraordinarily gifted beings, and others would not notice if their eternal self struck them in the face.

In 2016 angel Hate, who is my friend, is a twenty-eight year old single mother with one daughter. As Archangel of the epoch mission to earth known as The Gemini Star, I can tell you her family was sent on purpose by intent, and through His design and creation. She and her four brothers and sisters arrived between June 1, 1983 and June 2, 1988. The fact that her sister was born a Gemini 06/01/1983, and that Hate was born a Gemini 06/02/1988 may appear as a coincidence to you, but it appears as a signal, and a miracle for me. I don't live in a random accidental life; I exist along a perfect path. I am born 06/03/1963; so together the star looks like 06/01, 06/02, and then 06/03. As Hate spiraled into my world at work in human resources, and was eventually even seated directly next to me; it took only a couple of days to find God's birthday star, and understand that meeting her was not an accident, but is a coincidence. When you have spent your life looking for stars, then the 06/01, 06/02, 06/03 birthdates, cannot be ignored; ignoring God at age fifty-three is no more an option than ignoring God at age three. This star, and the angel it delivered, creates some mystery; we will wait for one day to see if there is a key to unlock the mystery.

Love Him, praise Him, fear Him; look for Him, and don't be shocked when He brings you unexpected things.

When angel Fury met angel Hate in early June 2015; Fury was already writing The Gospel of Fury: The Gemini Star. Hate's super power though was not made clear until March 10, 2016. The ability to identify an angelic superpower is a gift from God, and necessary to function as archangel of an earthly mission. Without being able to see God's framework of practical existence delivered into the world; you just really don't know what you know. Day after day the learning takes hold; then you know you must and can serve His purpose since He gave you the necessary tools as gifts. Gifts are not always for fun and happiness; gifts are necessary to get the job done; gifts are not nice targets for sarcasm; gifts are great targets for skeptics, so follow the trails left by mortal lives to discover the gifted lives behind the mission to substantiate Gods practicality.

Hate's brothers and sisters were born one after the other in heavenly minutes between 1983 and 1988. Their father was a one shot wonder; an angel sent for a single purpose. Hate's father apparently had just one main mortal objective, besides providing angelic love and angelic nurturing for the family; his main objective was to father the children, and then return back to God and heaven.

Angel Hate's dad passed away unexpectedly in April 2005 in Las Vegas while on vacation without his family. It had always been a dream of his to visit Las Vegas; he ended up leaving from Las Vegas, and returning to God and heaven. He had long suffered from diabetes, and although he was cleared to take the vacation, he did get sick. What killed him though, according to my understanding, was a lack of treatment at a local hospital. He died alone in a corridor on a gurney, according to my friend. I believe she hates that he left her at age sixteen going on seventeen; and her father's leaving her may be the hardest thing she thing she will ever have to hate. It may just be, when you loose your father at such a young age that is all the angelic learning you can take for one lifetime. She is loved at work, and is the nicest of people. She cannot bear to feel hate or show dislike. That is her practical life story to tell one day.

Angel Hate was sixteen, and living in Connecticut when her father passed away. She is blessed with the burden of angelic learning. She serves heavenly purpose; including learning everything about the human emotion of hate. She is very nice to know, and a great friend. The karma that surrounds her attempts to throw issues of hate in her direction to help her learn her angelic duty. She brushes off hate and awkwardness like a duck brushes water off its back. When she eventually passes, she will return to God a more knowledgeable creature, and serve being in the Kingdom of Light heavenly day after heavenly day. Hate is not so popular in heaven; not too common in life either; hate has much natural purpose, and is an important matter, albeit fleeting.

Love God, praise God, fear God; don't waste your energy hating; it won't last long.

Angel Hate has a strong mortal presence matched by a serious spiritual presence, along with a dutiful religious conviction. I tell her just enough about my writing to keep her interested and close, so that if there is ever a key to uncover mystery, we will be prepared, and she will have basic knowledge of her heavenly heritage. We may all pass through creation; not all of us have a special mission. She and her family belong to the Gemini Star mission. I told her I hoped to meet her family someday.

She cannot really see design, creation, and purpose just like the archangel of the modern gospel, because these kinds of progressive angelic events are rare events, and people are just not ready to have real life heavenly messengers showing up in their lives to start spreading gospel through the telling of angelic stories.

Angel Hate is young, intuitive, and spiritually gifted. Her existence and ultimate purpose is divinely inspired by design, and she is intentionally sent by God. She came through creation to help inspire this story, and to ensure the stories level of passion is what the Supreme Being wanted. God only knows what lies ahead in our future.

PART TWO

The Twelve Angels

SECTION I

Angel Jealousy

THE FIRST BORN FAMILY MEMBER WITHIN THE ANGELIC CORE IS THE angel Jealousy. She was born in 1938, and lives today as this story is being written. She is burdened with angelic learning, and blessed with long mortal life. All twelve members of the familial core of angels on earth live at the telling of this story. The time may come for the person to provide witness to the events and circumstances that resulted in the telling of this modern gospel, or not.

Blessed is her angelic life and sent by God for specific purpose; she leads our way into this mortal existence, and starts this mission from heaven. The familial core of twelve angels served to transform Fury's simple being into its lightened existence. Through lightened existence Fury is able to understand God's greater purpose, and to interpret each of the specific angelic messages that are necessary for the delivery of the gospel.

Through his lightening Fury is able to see and present the specific knowledge to create mankind's perspective to enable understanding. God desires Fury to treat humanity gently, with patience, to make it easier for man to swallow the modern testament; He provided a host of angelic beings to support the mission and encourage its success.

An angel's own confused perception of itself may contribute to a life filled with elusive understanding of the power of God's true creation, which is an actual angel on earth. You may prefer to think of angels on earth as messengers from heaven. Call them angels or call them messengers; with certainty they are rarely known and almost never presented so clearly and cleverly. Yes, God and heaven do much work inside earth's paradise of mortal existence.

The search for self awareness is a common pursuit of mankind, and in that way angels on earth are just like everyone else. Your own troubled search for identity may lead you to believe you are angelic in nature; and since you are headed in that direction anyway, practice makes perfect since there is no shortage of jobs in heaven. Some like to be; some like to serve; everyone can have what they want in God's Kingdom of Light. Practice does make perfect; get practice started in life, act like an angel, and spread joy through service; it's a good thing.

Angelic lightening is uncommon and no small thing; it is the result of His continual and gentle empowerment. Patiently He spends a lifetime lightening the messenger to its being, and finally the being can see His intent and purpose. His mystery remains mysterious, and angels especially seek His guidance.

The lightening of the messenger before the world brings God's angelic being to its arisen position between heaven and earth for humanity to see and watch. Heaven and earth then exist closely for just enough time to share in His intent and purpose. This is His dream for reality; to share His intent and purpose through unity of spiritual direction between heaven and earth for just a brief moment of time every once in a while.

This time is God's time; this is His great gift of presence for global humanity; He shepherds us now clearly for a special passing of the first epoch of man. It has been two thousand years since time began, and the day when the son walked the earth. One heavenly day passes around only once a lifetime. So, if the average human life is around seventy-five years, then it has only been a month of heavenly time since the son came to earth on his heavenly mission. We honor the son, when we honor the passing of the first epoch.

Think about this for a moment: one of heaven's years, which is twelve heavenly months, does equal just around twenty-four thousand earth years; who knows how long the earth will last; God knows. There is a long future ahead of humanity filled with pitfalls and disasters that the shepherd has to plan for. There is as much work done in heaven in just one heavenly year as man will do in twenty-four thousand years; billions and billions of eternal beings working and existing at the speed of light; resting as well, all beings have to rest, restless beings are careless beings (24,000 mortal years equals twelve epochs).

During the first epoch humanity progressed from scarce parchment to ubiquitous smart phones; slow down. Have some respect; feed the hungry, prevent suffering, stop persecution. Answer prayers for relief. Accept that God is good enough to ask for help; accept that heaven is good enough to ask for relief for those who are hardest to hear. Give an angel a break, and lend a helping hand.

Gospel is gospel for a reason; heavenly truth is truth when it is plain enough to see and presented clearly enough to understand; His word is as special as this time; celebrate this gospel, and celebrate the son as well as the Father, and plan for the future.

For one man alone to embrace his eternal presence during his mortal life, and see his role as God's messenger, is a significant spiritual event in itself. Such angelic lightening is lonely and no small step for that one man; full and complete lightening is the larger leap for mankind toward embracing eternity warmly, and turning in acknowledgment to seek God's intent, and understanding purpose as it is presented by the knowing messenger. These steps into knowing can take years of patient learning; God provides His teaching individually; God will shine His greater light for the world to see if we wait patiently.

He teaches reality when He provides reasonable facts of life, including birth dates and dates of death, reasoning, symbolism, and even scientific detail which we can ascertain as His stars and His keys, that have been delivered to clear up mystery. Stars and keys help create certainty within the reality of a world He has been crafting for centuries in preparation for this moment. He uses promise and hope to teach when we bridge history, tradition, myth and popular belief and understanding into this self-evident gospel.

For today's mission and the life of Fury, He provides the birth date 6/3/63 which Fury then understands is the number of the biblical beast 666 by adding the two threes together to get six. The number of the biblical beast is a teaching tool, and a learning star, and becomes your key to unlock mystery to affirm His presence. God gave all the necessary things for this mission; no thing is to be wasted since all the things add up to make sense of His intelligence. Waste not; want not; what more could you want for; just let me know; we wait together for the miracle which you seek; it will come sooner rather than later.

Teaching tools and learning stars include items like the upside down crucifix representing the popular symbol of the anti-Christ, except the Supreme Being taught Fury to pick up that inverted cross, and use it as the sword of God rising from the earth. God showed Fury to let the sword rising out of the earth wantonly symbolize God's desire for justice and admit His presence mightily. There lay the existing thing, the inverted cross; God empowers it then to become His mighty sword rising up for Fury to behold and then embrace strongly. Fury labels the sword of God in a positive light, and then your needed knowledge is delivered so the world of man can embrace unity of spirit and direction heading toward His vision of humanity including the future of a fearless freedom in belief and worship.

This is the goal of the gospel; to demonstrate God's power which delivers His presence, and leads you into accepting His modern intent and evident purpose since once in a while He has to clear things up just a little bit; no major overhaul required.

Along the path of learning we will continually witness God filling the wheel barrow of knowledge so that the weight of the evidence results in the modern testament delivered convincingly through the gospel stories of Fury. This story contains His fury delivered gently for the world of mankind to embrace. The World of Make Believe provides more than enough reasoning to remove doubt, and to create belief in today's modern prophecy delivered in time for the passing of the first epoch into the second epoch.

Consider the calendar and June 3rd, 1963, and recognize that this gospel comes at the changing of the epoch which is coincident with the start of the second millennia. He designed it simply so you could simply understand it. You can see that the Supreme Being did not have a lot of dates to work with if Fury was to reach lightening at just the right age and moment in history. So, June 3, 1963 was the perfect date to be born. Thank God, thank heaven and creation, and my parents Understanding and Faith. Thank the stars that light the way to discovery, and thank the Sainted Pope John XXIII as well for his star of passing June 3, 1963 which helps clear up mystery through affirmation of possibility.

From birth in 1963 to inner lightening in 2014, Fury's life shifted into high gear with sight and understanding of the signaling delivered through the Gemini Star which is represented by the real lives of angel Spite's twin Gemini daughters born on May 26, 1966 coinciding in the birth, to the day three years later, of her Gemini son angel Peace May 26, 1969.

The stars shown within the threes are especially for me, as I am also arisen on the third day of June, this adds mystery and points toward the resurrection of the son of God on the third day. Through His design and creation God alludes to the presence of the son in the being of Fury's life. Alas, you will be left in illusion there for in that regard I remain a paltry messenger of his word in an angelic life designed only to bear simple witness to the greatness of the Father. Here you see the straightforward delivery and simple reasoning behind the sudden presence of the fallen angel which includes the powerful yet alarming anti-Christ symbolism. I am no Christ child, just a simple notepad for God to scrawl a quick message to man. When I am gone, though, you will scratch your head in wonderment and unknowing, but that is by His design to reach His purpose. Fury's only real hope is to return to the embrace of our proud heavenly Father who may be satisfied with a successful earthly mission and possible legacy.

I do allude to the possibility and personal desire to see the birth of any Grand Child of the First Epoch of God. This He shows to Fury through our tears of joy and also of sorrow; those tears are for you to wonder over and dream about. It is pleasing to the heart to see the vision of the grand kid, knowing the child will not come into poverty, and is only to be admired and loved during life. The children of God are His legacy, and serve heaven more than earth; earth gives the eternal existence much needed balance. The great things promised to man are already contained in these original gospel stories, and there is no necessity to expect further evidence of His majesty and love for humanity; do not anticipate that kids will bring more than the Father already delivered. He will not ask for more until He has what he needs; that's prophecy.

Knowing now what you have read, you know His love extends to using His power to correct man's course in knowing, even to the point of demonstrating His control through creation of generations of men. He can shape humanity plainly through one man and through control of multitudes of men generationally. He has the power to deliver what He wants into the world. It is up to humanity to accept what is plainly given; sharing is caring especially between heaven and earth.

Fear God, praise God, and love God; certainly be aware of the power that belongs to God the Father and the Supreme Being.

It is through the Archangel of the First Epoch that the possibility of the Grand Child of God exists. It is this celebratory path through the gospel where the changing of the epoch can deliver a legacy to be loved on earth, and become admitted in heaven. The second gospel describes the possibility, but avoids the probability of the grandchildren. So, now you can see, and now you can know, how the world of mankind in reality can lead to legacy admitted in heaven, and how the legacy becomes whole through the unity of knowledge between heaven and earth. Sounds pretty far fetched; yet here the Archangel has laid it at your feet, and asks you to wonder and dream. This is one reason we call the second story of the trilogy The Gospel of Fury: The World of Make Believe. You can have it your way today; men, women and children of the epoch; you need only know that earthly things make heavenly things whole.

The Archangel knows what to do with popularity. He only needs the tools of commerce to take care of his family, and to be left in peace to write, and to teach the gospel. God gave all things to the single being, including the ability to administer teaching and deliver the warmth of charm to point out and demonstrate God's path into reality through the modern Gospel of Fury. We just need a safe campus and classroom, which in today's world is apparently a lot to ask for with all the school shootings we know about. It would be a tragic conclusion to our story to be gunned down in a classroom; then again, that would be in public instead of in a field surrounded by strangers. The frightening thing is not dying; the frightening thing is dying alone.

The twin daughters of angel Spite who represent the Gemini Star are not yet named angels, since I have never met them, so I do not know their super powers. Pray they are blessed with lives of learning, for angels sent into the earth and not sent to learn, do not live long.

Maybe it is hard to see what I say when I say I see a star. Star light star bright, the star I see is the star that is sent. Twin Gemini unnamed angelic girls born 5/26 then given away at birth followed by a Gemini named angel brother three years later to the day 5/26 is a star given by God. You can accept His creation; as He provides it by design; just to show He can and did provide the knowledge through real life demonstration. The archangel finds God's stars, you use the keys I present to fill your minds eye with possibility.

In 2014 angel Fury discovered one of his gifts was the ability to know the angelic super powers of his family members who are the core angels of the Gemini Star mission at the changing of the epoch. The family members with super powers are named angels since Fury uses God's gift to recognize the angelic burden each family member brings with them through creation.

One by one over my life, I have been uncovering their secret, or not so secret, eternal identities. If you were to ask them the truth, they may not see it clearly; their purpose is to support the mission, along with the story presented by the archangel. The archangel owes them his very being and lightening; after lightening and forever after they are the responsibility of the fully lightened archangel; to fail them is to fail God and man. Archangel Fury will not fail God or his responsibility to his mortal and eternal families.

My eldest aunt is the angel Jealousy. Angels are not merely named Michael, Rafael, or Peter. Christian names do not organize being nor facilitate bureaucracy or perform any real eternal function and are just not practical; God includes practicality by design. Christian names are for the living; existence and the performance of duty are for every being; all of our purpose is to serve within the necessity of functionality. Look around you now within your earthly paradise, and you can witness the fully functional universe starting with the earth, and reaching beyond the stars into our eternal heavenly home that does hold God's promise of being. You can believe in that heavenly home; you can wait and see it for yourself; you will have it your way in heaven; one heavenly way or another you will make it through heaven's gate. The eventuality of passing is no mystery, and your heavenly welcome is assured; this was God's original promise of salvation.

Things like jealousy do not exist naturally in eternity which is the Kingdom of Light; such things including jealousy must be maintained by design to support eternal being, to facilitate the bureaucracy of heaven, and to make God happy.

Issue resolution is as real in heaven as it is on earth. In fact, some heavenly issues require mortal intervention; some worldly problems benefit from heavenly intervention; being supports both time on earth, and existence in eternity. Angels support all things, because that is how God administers the universe in an organized manner even if it is as far away as eternity which reaches into reality.

To suggest that God is disorganized is to suggest the universe is disorganized, and we plainly see that it is clearly organized and can be described scientifically. The eternal side of reality and the reality side of reality coexist closer than you might imagine and understand. Being reaching across eternity into time, though, is a privilege reserved for special purpose described by the Supreme Being; otherwise we would exist in chaos. That is gospel.

God uses angels, including Jealousy, to administer His bureaucracy in heaven, and to help the earth and man through the power of prayer along with intelligent thinking. Sometimes praying directly to an angel will help your thinking; especially when you focus on the real issue troubling your mortal life.

Angels are here to help. Often, an angel will watch over your shoulder and can help you through the strength of your own eternal being. Knowledge and understanding are attributes shared in reality, and increased by the power of eternal awareness. Do not be alarmed by your own eternal knowledge of being since this will help you reach an increased level of intelligence. Your own intelligence brings you closer to Him, and the path you create together.

Heaven's path is the simpler path to the intelligent understanding of God's universe in reality which includes humanity. Most of your eternal understanding outside of the world of reality will come to you naturally when you pass; this is His promise to humanity, and is the essence of the Holy Grail. The grail is the cup containing forgiveness that is freely given to man through the bond between the Father and the son. Ask your brothers and sisters to forgive you today; rest assured in eternal forgiveness; live wisely to maintain a short day of judgment. Shared time in judgment with those you wronged or were wronged by can make for a long afternoon; the best we can hope for is commonly shared wisdom during our lifetimes, and lots of healthy life savings.

God demonstrated angel Jealousy's identity for this gospel and the important mission of our time. There is no reason to expound much further on her required role as a learner. She must learn in life what she can in regard to all things impacting the emotional activities that result in the feelings or experiences concerning jealousy or even jealous rage.

Jealousy is related to the fear of loss. Jealousy is a powerful emotional condition, and can certainly become a dangerous thing when it is out of control. Unfortunately jealousy is not something we can easily control. The fear of emotional loss and support is incredibly alarming to us as human beings. Jealousy can even cause a human heart to seize suddenly, and stop beating as it normally does.

My aunt, angel Jealousy, also happens to be the mother of my cousin angel Hope. Hope was born a Gemini, of course, on June 15, 1967. Hope is now deceased. Readers of The Gemini Star will remember that angel Hope was a dear person in life, but Hope was left hopeless in life by design. Fury is an ancient soul and blind. Hope is passed away now, waiting between earth and heaven to guide Fury safely back to God's kingdom whenever the eventuality of passing takes place for Fury. God shows His benevolence for Fury when He provides for a real life angelic guide to bring the being of blind Fury back to the gates of heaven safely. God is good.

My aunt Jealousy has suffered great loss during her lifetime. It is true that her first husband, Hope's father, more likely than not, died of jealousy when my aunt angel Jealousy removed the presence of her love from his life. It was within a few years following their separation that my uncle passed away alone at home. He had every reason to live, but a broken heart can kill even those that are the most filled with being while they are alive. He maintained a valuable career in sales, which came naturally to him. He was gifted with amazing children, as most of us are. He is admired greatly to this day by all his family. He was beloved in life, and exists now close to the Kingdom of Heaven, grateful to have been released from his own mortal burden, and God's mission.

My uncle's son, angel Hope, having lost His father, whom he loved, lost just enough hope, and then abandoned life as we know it. Angel Hope fulfils immortal desire now, and is probably enjoying the telling of this gospel across my shoulder. Angels are always near and dear to our hearts.

Angel Jealousy's heavenly learning takes place within her mortal mind and heart, and is hopefully retained in her life savings as she feels and possibly contemplates the incredibly debilitating helplessness that jealousy can inflict, and understands that the resulting emotional heartache can result in heart attack. The angel's mortal learning facilitates its role in heaven as a servant of God and all beings.

There is no thing that occurs in nature that is not real in heaven as well. Heaven is not life though, heaven is the Kingdom of Light, heaven is as good as dreaming. We can all be thankful God had the foresight to keep things organized, and did structure His heavenly bureaucracy with knowing angels ready to assist being both on earth, and in heaven.

The twelve angels that are within the core of my family, which is our mission, serve to lighten being and fulfill purpose. By witnessing their existence and discovering each identity, I am lightened. A family of angels on earth is provided to assist the archangel, or chief angel, become who he must become in order to author this rare gospel, and give the words God wants given.

Without twelve angels to provide their keys to unlock mystery, Fury would not have seen the light. Without twelve angels on guard with meaning and purpose, Fury may have thrown caution to the wind, and been left in danger without enough understanding to know fear. Without twelve angels with specific messages, part of the testament may have been overlooked, and mankind would have been left lacking a part of what God intends for world of today. It is God who sent the mission as it is; Fury's duty was only to tell you what He did.

We know He is good when He enables understanding to create knowing. Angel Jealousy provides an earthly message to all four corners of God's earthly paradise. God abhors jealousy among religions and within spirituality. God allows for a world of tradition and history, and for any approach that brings men closer to Him and His kingdom in goodness.

The good Lord specifically designed the participation of angel Jealousy for today's earthly mission. The message to the archangel is to beware. Be wary of man's jealous nature. Keep on guard as you enter into the world of mankind with God's modern gospel. People may not want to embrace gospel for it is not specifically written for them, but was written for everyone.

Mankind's propensity toward a jealous nature may cause him to make some attempt to contaminate the message and meaning of the modern gospel. Do not be jealous of this testament in any corner of the world; do your best to spread the gospel and embrace His goodness in showing us the light in our existence. He is demonstrating His desire to continue on in progress with us; do not leave God out of progress; human progress is shaped by the shepherd more than we can know in these short earthly lives. Luckily for you, you have a story to help you see His way.

SECTION II

Angel Understanding

THROUGH THE RAINBOW OF CREATION, USING CLEVER DESIGN, GOD delivered the angel Understanding into the world in 1940. Dad is the second child born within his generation. Just heavenly minutes apart, he followed his big sister angel Jealousy into this world as part of The Gemini Star mission. He has been a commander of men, and has spent a lifetime searching for philosophical truth and studying its meaning. He has always been, and still remains, the kindest of dads.

The immortal being of angel Understanding was God's selection of a supernatural existence that we currently know as an angel on earth while it still lives. He regrets that he will run out of time and pass away. It fits that angel Fury, who carries the heart of the truest believer, was born to the angels Understanding and Faith. Once more, for the record, this is not Fury making up a story for fun and profit. This is the writing of a mortal being gifted by God to interpret what God sent to demonstrate His own power and intelligence. I. B. Fury would never have been so clever as to create these characters and story lines. This is God's gospel, and these are Fury's words; I am acting as a scribe as best I can interpret desire and meaning at the crossroad of mankind, family, and heaven.

God shows us His perfect design through creation when he provides a father who would allow his imaginative son to grow up into a free thinking man capable of willingly recognizing universal spirituality, deciphering relative truth, and connecting pertinent fact, so that he could then author the modern testament intending to reach across all the points of God's globe of humanity; those are big shoes to fill for a kid who grew up outside the church.

Angel Understanding lacks commitment to his immortal soul, and fosters a lack of belief in the Supreme Being. His open denial of spiritual existence is his mortal demonstration, fulfilling his eternal requirement toward learning what he can about humanity's understanding of existence within God's universe. To have grown up within the church, and be highly educated, yet lack understanding of the very God who created him, and sent him into the world of time, represents the perfection in God's design for the angel on earth who lacks understanding.

Karma is the powerful thing affecting all of us, but especially angelic being. Karma exerts the forces of nature and coincidence onto the life of the angelic being to deliver situations that forcibly enable angelic learning, and can lead to angelic lightening over time. Some of these guidelines and rules are supplied as forward looking teaching tools to aid understanding while there is the chance to deliver the simple truth. The future is coming; things may not always be as clear as they are presented here; God's messengers will arrive as He plans; so learn while you can.

My dad understands most things; just not God. You just cannot make up a story better than to have an angel representing the heart of understanding who does not know or understand his soul, and God's intention to preserve it. Dad will probably reach the gates of heaven and avoid the shock of suddenly knowing when he remembers that God designed it all simply in order to keep it foolproof. The things that matter to God and heaven are your life savings, so keep those intact. Do not worry about a rule book for soul maintenance during life, and do not worry over whether or not you will find your way to the gates of heaven; just worry about keeping it all together; God always had the journey and the basics covered; He's got your back; always did. Don't take my word for it; trust in God.

It is only the oblivious soul who risks flying apart at heaven's gate when suddenly knowing full well the power of God, and the reality of the Kingdom of Light; atheism and agnosticism are ancient and fine systems of belief, they are embraced by God within His commitment to freedom of belief and worship, and through the covenant he maintains with man; man is good enough. Skepticism is good; questioning opens the heart to possibility; possibility is not oblivion; sarcasm is pointless.

Only oblivion enables a soul to loose its concentration at the gates long enough to fall apart. Not to worry, you don't even need to call the repairmen, the watch angels at the gates of heaven will have an eternal team of experts on hand to put being and life savings back together again, and you will be on your way. Humpty Dumpty never had it as good as you will when you die, and travel back through creation. God kept it fool proof for good reason.

There is no man I know who has God's footsteps more plainly visible throughout his life than my father. He lacks belief, though, in something as central and essential to our universe as eternity and eternal being. This represents his lack of understanding during mortality, but it does place the heart of Understanding within complete compliance with God's mortal objective for an eternal being burdened with facing a life of learning.

Angel Understanding is the second of the twelve angels to provide a message to the Archangel to add to the success of the mission, and to help keep the Archangel on point. The message of Understanding to the Archangel is to show kindness to men. Angel Fury, the embodiment of the furious heart, will endeavor to remember that mankind's level of understanding is based on the time it takes him to grow into any willingness to accept newly acquired knowledge that may be slightly different when compared to the old knowledge he maintained so faithfully for so long.

Given enough time, man will grow to understand even the most improbable of events. In this case, the improbable event is God reaching into the world, together with a bunch of angels. In particular, the self described Archangel proclaiming this the age of a changing epoch for mankind. Fresh gospel sent to increase knowledge and enhance understanding, and also to affirm freedom of belief based on God's desire to maintain diversity, even when backed up by what God can provide, in the way of His visible design and puzzle pieces which were placed together through His intelligent creation, may just be a little hard to understand on first consideration. If you suffer some indigestion, take something for it, get a good nights sleep; then consider it again; just don't walk away.

Understanding, and admitting that this writing is God's modern truth, is a challenge presented by <u>The Gospel of Fury</u>. The challenge is for man to weigh the evidence of the lives of Fury and his company, and to understand that this gospel contains what God can provide to increase the probability of belief, because story-telling on its own is not good enough when the target audience is wise, and it will require more than faith to consider progressive teaching.

A further challenge of the gospel is to admit that even if we may understand and believe that the words contain truth based on consistent story lines and the real lives God provided, that the truth then is after all God's truth, and not merely coincidence arranged by the imaginative nature of the writer. The accumulating weight of the factual evidence presented as heavenly coincidence is measurable, and may still increase since this is real time prophecy. It must be admitted that it is amazing that the factual coincident evidence exists in the one life of Fury, and that it is organized and presented clearly; you can believe in an accidental universe; or you can embrace God's universe, and accept His progressive ideal sent for a modern world.

For modern reasoning concerning God's word, this is the gospel you want to work with; this gospel will carry man into the future; a time will come when heaven again provides something clearly. Modern reasoning, including logical conclusion, allows for the understanding that God would necessarily provide support for testimony, so that testimony alone does not necessarily have to create and maintain understanding and belief; you don't have to rely on faith alone when you have good evidence.

Complete mission success based on overwhelming truth and evidence is needed so that His modern touch is felt without too much doubt. For the world to have overlooked His word at the two-thousand year anniversary of the beginning of time, at the moment when the son walked the earth, is what should have alarmed us, if we had indeed been anticipating his return. No reason for concern; the word of God arrived exactly on time.

There is a worldwide collective leap of faith necessary, since successfully adapting fresh knowledge requires admitting to new understanding globally, of divine reach and power. The collective popularity the Archangel seeks is a long shot for mankind, since the writing was provided by a white American who is closely aligned to the European Christian description of the son. The son's message has always included all of humanity, and God's true benevolence embraces all forms of belief including the entire historic legacy that God enjoys Himself; check with Him in heaven concerning specifics if you have concerns; He is the one God; He has time for everybody, surprising as it seems; then again He does have eternity to get it all done.

The son was present when calendar time started recording years, and that time started for everyone at the same time. It is 2016 all across the globe today as this story is being written. The changing of the epoch is the change of the epoch for everyone, and God is the God of everyone; so there is no explanation required when we all love God, and show gratitude for His benevolent and forgiving nature by embracing the globes tradition and history in affirmation through togetherness to demonstrate unity of direction toward God; the branches of the tree indeed spread from the trunk.

The modern story is not directed at a specific religion, because God is the Supreme Being of all beings, and shepherds all of humanity through all of belief, which is headed toward the one God.

Have faith in the messenger; a simple and faithful messenger calling him self I. B. Fury. The life of Fury is central to all the things God intended for the mission. Two-thousand years after the son of God walked the earth along comes the necessary Archangel of the First Epoch giving away the pearls of wisdom the Supreme Being provided.

It sounds improbable that a man could write the word of God to achieve His desired modern objective; yet, if it is God's will, there will be no denying success; so it is probably okay to set aside initial doubt, and accept the reality of the situation as it is presented, and work collectively to consider the possibility by admitting some hope into your heart; that remains relevant only if you have been waiting, and you hope <u>The Gospel of Fury</u> is the real thing.

Whenever man can briefly set aside dogma, and be open to contemplation, then all things are possible. A little togetherness, through reasoning is not too much to ask, and is not beyond the capability of mankind; great ideas brought at great times deserve great effort, and may require a little sacrifice; the little sacrifice may only involve admitting to the possibility of a modern gospel.

You are being asked to consider a progressive leap in practical ideology that is roughly the same size as changing from 1960s technology to present day technology; worldwide progression toward unity in spirit; freedom of belief; salvation with forgiveness for all; no terror and no war in God's name. This is just a minor tune up across the globe, albeit performed by heavenly technicians; no real change for any special group; don't just speak for God, speak for yourself; just don't limit access to heaven; don't fight wars and don't commit terrorism. Easy enough, and who on earth would want to disagree with any of these progressive things; they each sound like understandably good things we can acknowledge and use to enhance man's free will. God's central mission was to remove some doubt in His goodness; dwindling doubt among men is easily achieved when man even considers the objectives presented in this gospel; no major tune up needed; just open up your heart to possibility; time will deliver the known truth and heaven will shine in success; God will be happy, and spread joy.

Love God; praise God; fear God; understand God willingly and wholeheartedly whenever He is presented plainly, honestly, and when it feels like His truth is real; if you don't feel it, don't make believe. It is Fury's job to deliver The World of Make Believe; so don't fake belief, don't fake faith, don't act like you know anything if you don't; and trust that you won't be faked out, either.

SECTION III

Angel Faith

MY MOTHER, ANGEL FAITH, WAS BORN IN 1941. SHE ENTERTAINS neither faith nor belief in God. She is ambivalent in regard to a Supreme Being and heavenly kingdom, except that they are imaginative ideas, and are good subject matter for man's artistic creations. She will deny that she is lacking in any way. She openly proclaims that her lack of faith represents only the reality of the world in which she lives. The air we breathe is the air the planet provides thanks to the cosmos alone, and when we breathe no more we are simply passed away, and that's the end of that. Her approach toward life is pragmatic and based on the visible existence we can see and measure; that is enough for life.

Things appear to be going quite well for mother Faith; she just does not need or desire faith or belief in a God to live her life; she harbors no questions over any eternal bliss or a resting place for any lighted being or soul. The argument here would be that God has indeed burdened the mortal being with the eternal task of learning the ins and outs of man's commitment to a Supreme Being who created the world, and possibly the universe, and also offers mortal forgiveness and eternal salvation. That is just a little too much for her.

I assure my mother that when she passes she will pass to the gates of heaven, and that her lighted soul will return to God; she insists that she does not need it or need to believe it, and would not maintain any faith in it. Her ardent denial of the after life and God, has always been clear; it took little time for her son, the future Archangel of the First Epoch of Humanity, to clearly see her super power was faith itself. My knowledge of her unnatural denial of faith took shape years and years ago, and probably was a cornerstone in the development of my understanding of my own eternal purpose. She edits these words objectively for her son, and scoffs at the possibility that her son has any possibility of being correct, and that he only maintains a great imagination. This is an instant where we hope mother does not know best.

Mother is blessed with the burden of learning and long life. She has indeed discovered faith, and continually studies faith, whenever she enjoys what man is capable of while he preserves and enhances images or thoughts demonstrating his understanding or individual interpretation of his own identity and position in the vast universe of existence. Mankind is uniquely positioned to be representative of his commitment to himself including the ideals of life's experience, and this is what he presents in his artwork and literature, and this is where the angel Faith discovered faith.

Mother found, and thoroughly enjoys, humanity's faith in itself through its varied artistic accomplishments; unwittingly and without knowing it, she does study faith and therefore completes her angelic burden of learning. We don't need for her to admit it to God in order to appreciate it; which is good because she will deny it was any angelic commitment sent with her from creation. Pondering faith includes thinking about man's art, and that is real enough for God since faith belongs to man uniquely.

Faith is strong; karma is a friend of faith and long ago abandoned any opposition to faith.

The angel Faith's eternal being has seemingly reached into her mortal self and accomplished what God desired. God desires His angels on earth to learn. Learned angels are one of God's requirements for the bureaucracy of heaven to function. Without learned angels in heaven, problems would not be resolved, and heavenly beings would not always be happy, or have what they wanted the way He wanted. Life includes suffering enough; heaven is just for enjoyment; this is how God intended things to exist, and to be understood.

Without learned angels, mortal prayers will fall on God's shoulders alone, and He has a lot going on. Go ahead and pray to an angel for help, it will increase your own intelligence and comprehension; God appreciates it when heaven is put to the task. The Supreme Being is a task master above all else, His great joy is in accomplishment, His fondest desire is to have the paradise of earth exist closer to the reality of heaven, and this includes knowing heaven is here to help.

You can imagine a God who wants you to know He wants to work closely in togetherness with you so your path with Him is smoother; that is the reality He wants you to know. God really does care enough, and He clearly wants to help out more plainly; bureaucracy is not always bad, especially when it is God's bureaucracy.

Her angelic message to her son, angel Fury, is to protect man's faith. Faith includes believing with a strong backbone, and praying with a clenched fist, and clenched heart. True faith is when man believes with enough courage and conviction to take risks and create action that could result in change or loss. If the risks you take are safe, then they may not be risky enough to create much change.

If life and faith required no apparent change, would heaven then be reaching into the world to enhance faith through gospel? Protecting faith includes keeping faith in the forefront of man's image of himself, and the path the shepherd is clearing; challenging the world's religions and spirituality to work together; united to admit the modern gospel is risky, and is a demonstration of faith in God's purpose.

Faith and belief are some of the things we lived with in the first epoch. To have faith is to attempt to live without doubt. From the beginning of time, throughout the first epoch of man, we have maintained belief and faith that there is a God and heaven; we can know better now that there is a God and heaven in modern times through the gospel of our modern age, albeit presented out of His growing fury.

Have faith that God knows when we abuse each other in His name, that abuse in His name upsets Him. Have faith and trust in one another; allow one another to live and worship freely in liberty; kill one another if you desire; no longer kill in the name faith in God; that is God's rule.

From the first epoch of mankind's childhood into the second epoch of manhood is the journey the modern gospel describes and assures us is real. The gospel includes the details you need in manhood, facts you do not have to accept on faith alone. There are details which are His stars and keys from creation. He enjoys sending details along our path of understanding to enhance your faith in His goodness.

Our faith is also how we practice our chosen belief, and fosters tradition often based on heritage. God enjoys a healthy faith-filled diverse system of belief across His globe. He does not require complete faith as a test to measure your love in order to gain acceptance with Him. God created being, and God does not waste what he created. Your individual practice of your faith, or even lack of practice, represents your uniqueness, and that makes you special to him, and delivers value to Him. Bring all your faith and tradition and heritage, and bring it toward Him; that is how we honor Him in the worldly way He desires. He has faith in you; He has faith in mankind; He does not need understanding to exist in any other way than in freedom of belief. Just keep an open heart; He likes to work His way in; that is His great pleasure.

The Gospel of Fury protects the faith of all mankind by admitting that God always showed great interest in a diversity of belief and worship over thousands and thousands of years of humanity's evolution. Protecting the practices and knowledge of faith includes protecting stories, ancient myth, astrology, historic tradition, the world's entire heritage and art, and is tantamount to God's desire for our path toward knowing His goodness, and maintaining mankind's individuality; destruction of His history contributes to His level of fury.

Love God, praise God, fear God; let's not contribute to His increasing level of fury.

Heaven is the space where light takes shape. Light is the true energy of the universe that God uses to create existence out of nothingness. All of God's desire is useless unless He shares His power through real existence. Light is His tool in eternity to maintain existence and being; knowing souls are His great joy and His paradise. The paradise of earth only maintains human being as long as time permits. God never intended a limited amount of time to enjoy His relationships with beings; it is only worldly planets that contain life where time is real, and being is therefore strictly limited by nature.

Light is not life, and a complete being cannot be lighted alone. Light is the power of the universe, but light alone cannot create unique character, and special nature. Mortal existence separates our nature and builds our character which is translated into our valuable life savings, and maintained in our being also known as our soul. A cookie cutter existence of being could not maintain the joy God desires for heaven. God decided eons ago that He enjoyed experience, and that predictability was dull. God grew into knowing that the unpredictable nature of individual life would provide for the completeness of the universe he was building.

His creations became those things that we can now describe and measure with science, and model with mathematics. These real things, including life, are supported within reality; His great creations include those things that we cannot measure now, but that exist throughout eternity, including within the reality of heaven. The reality of heaven, combined with the reality of a world that measures the passage of time, creates the universe of things that truly matter; stars are nice to ponder, comets are pretty to watch, and black holes are useful and frightening; existence is what truly matters, and only heaven and earth provide God the meaningful existence He seeks.

At the beginning, He began creating things, and He will keep on creating things, and changing things, for as long as He wants them to become more meaningful. The things that heaven needs are enhanced in life; being is shared by heaven and the world; your life savings are kept in your soul when your being passes through the gates of heaven; individuality is then maintained in heaven as it is on earth; and God experiences joy, and heaven shines.

The universe needs the limits of life and nature to supply the character God desires; being needs the eternal side of the lighted universe to supply the continuity of knowing that God enjoys. He does not actually enjoy loneliness, even though He maintains an elusive nature. You know as well as I, that to know Him in life is not always so easy; you and I also know that His joy is felt and known more easily in His Kingdom of Light.

We really do know more than we thought we knew; He knew more about what you would need to know than you understood He was willing to send; He gives you this depth of knowledge and reason to carry you far into the future.

You have lost enough words so far; do not lose these words; these words were sent carefully, and took planning; do not imagine He will not send His word again, with equal care and planning.

The great importance of faith includes understanding that God provided a complete universe, so that His sand box would never be empty of, or filled with, strangers. He likes a happy sandbox, a variety of playmates, and for His playmates to play happily together. It takes heaven and earth to supply proper meaning to existence and being, otherwise heaven and earth might end up in a cookie cutter design, and that would be dull for everyone. God does not like dull; so have a little faith in one another, and enjoy your variety of belief, faith and worship.

SECTION IV

Angel Spite

THE FOURTH ANGEL OF <u>THE GEMINI STAR</u> MISSION TO ARRIVE ON earth was born in 1944. Angel Spite is the third child to be born into her generation of our mortal family. She entered life following her sister angel Jealousy, who is my aunt, and her brother angel Understanding, who is my father.

Angel Spite has always been close to my mother, angel Faith, they remain friends today. They do not live close to one another, and my father is no longer married to my mother, but the hearts of Faith and Spite remain connected, since I am married to angel Spite's daughter, the angel that bears the heart of Redemption.

Of course I married my first cousin. Proximity of beings is central to God's plan for angels on earth to succeed in the things He sends them to do. I have always followed the path He lays for me. He laid the path from Fury to Redemption as clear as the asphalt highway runs from sea to shining sea.

Angelic missions sent into the world to deliver God's knowledge and to create human understanding may not work well without the Supreme Being sending His messengers into the same family. Unrelated messengers will remain clueless because understanding God's message will remain elusive and unconvincing. It takes time and evidence to convince men to act on His behalf; for men to act as angels on earth and to share burdens is no small task. It takes ever more evidence in a progressive world to boldly go where no men have gone before; angelic nature has now been declared on earth. When the messengers arrive in a family, the family grows in time together with spirit; then the message that there is a core of decipherable being becomes clear to the critical soul, who must piece it together. That soul that becomes convinced that it should, and will, tell the world, is a lightened soul, and may turn out to be archangel of an important mission into the world of man and time.

The angelic family originally is sent together, then stays together, growing as family, which gets God what He intended when He designed the mission, and created the mortality to deliver it.

I did not now on our wedding day, May 13, 1995 that we were living lives of prophecy, and that there was great purpose coming our way. I did know that it never felt right to consider marrying just anybody on earth. I always knew I would marry into a special relationship; cousin Redemption was a great choice.

When her daughter, angel Redemption, questioned her mother Spite concerning the wisdom in loving a first cousin, the queen mother of the mission shattered her doubt. The position Spite took with her daughter that day, laid one more stone onto God's path to celebrate the epoch. If Spite's eternal being and mortal self had lacked intent and purpose that day, then Fury and Redemption would not have married, and the earthly mission of the epoch might not have taken shape; The Gemini Star may never have risen. God does work in mysterious ways, so we cannot know for sure if we would have eventually gotten together without Spite's wisdom that day.

There are many forks in every road, so if you think you missed your turn, don't be surprised if you get to where you are going anyway; the turn you missed may have been the one God wanted you to miss.

There are accidents that make you imagine they happen on purpose, because of unintentional consequences that create good things; then there are consequences that happen because good things are intended. The day of that decision, angel Spite demonstrated no spite, but she did maintain her desire to see her children happy including allowing them the freedom to pursue happiness despite potential risks. As I said, angel Spite is the kindest of women, and I owe her debts I cannot repay in this lifetime, but I plan to after life.

Angel Spite is the queen mother of the <u>The Gemini Star</u> mission. As this gospel is being written, her eternal star now burns brighter than her mortal being permits. She bore the brunt of delivering the children that make up the core of the mission. The children are the angelic signaling stars providing God's shining details to give weight to the reality of His mission. She gave birth to the four angels at the close core of the family; along with the twin daughters, who with their brother Peace, are the signaling Gemini Star that shines over our mission. The world of mankind owes much to Spite; God owes much to Spite; I am sure she would say that thank you is good enough for now; that is the person who is my mother in law; thank God for her.

My aunt knows little of spite, and is the kindest mother. She allowed each of her four children, angel Redemption, angel Peace, angel Love, angel Doubt, to grow freely into God's design. She is a saint, and one of the nicest people I will ever know. She is indeed burdened with long life, and blessed with learning; but these are not great gifts; the greatest gift would be the gift the world owes her, which is peace. She deserves the peace in knowing her story, and the great works God sent into the world through her. Fury cannot give her the peace that the success of the gospel will deliver. When Fury laments over time, remember, the family core is aging out. They all still live in 2016; but anything can happen; real time prophecy using real lives means we are all watching as this story develops.

Angels can claim to be angels all day and all night long; prophecy can purport to be prophecy, until the cows come home; gospel can look like truth, and taste like truth, and smell like truth; but until the world consumes the gospel truth, and accepts the prophecy, then there is no real success, and no peace for the weary angelic souls waiting on an eternity they may not fully miss.

Practice being an angel today, spread a little gospel, share a little truth; tell your friends in the world of today that God's magic has returned to the world to deliver hope and confirm dreams, to honor the son, to honor all of the world's belief; to celebrate the passing of the first epoch of mankind. You are the men, women, and children of the first epoch living within the age of the passing of the epoch. Practice idealism today and celebrate today; imagine mankind one heavenly month from now; think how the men, women and children of the second epoch will look back on this day in two thousand years; ask yourself if you are giving them everything they will need to understand their role in their time.

Angel Spite's mortal life has been filled with labor and sacrifice. Her life came with suffering, hard choices, and difficult circumstance; she could write her own novel thanking God for a tough life. She has worked hard physically at home, and at her careers; she has encountered a karma filled lifetime of emotional turmoil learning to understand and know spite; she has been greatly loved by those around her, and returned that love; she has learned much in the way of controllable, and uncontrollable, human emotion. She will return to heaven and God with much wisdom to spread throughout the kingdom of eternal being.

God sends named mission angels in part to learn; the archangel watches and reports on their progress; heaven and earth exist closely in learning for just a short time, and this is a rare moment. Fury can place his hand on the bible, and swear to tell the truth, the whole truth, and nothing but the truth; Fury knows through his own witness, and promises, that every angel of the mission is learning valuable truth that will benefit God and kingdom, and that each of the mission angels are deserving of their long lives of burden, and that they will be blessed in healthy life savings when they return to the gates of heaven.

Praise Him; love Him; fear Him; learn for Him in everything you do; you can easily end up working for Him directly. Even with billions of souls, there is plenty of work; Muslim, Hindu, Christian, Buddhist, skeptic, whatever you want to practice; you choose to be or to serve once you make it back to the lighted kingdom; uniqueness with freedom of belief and plenty of work for anyone, that is His promise.

My understanding is that Spite's pregnancy with the twins, and their birth May 26, 1966 forced her into to a hard decision that has weighed heavily on her heart to this day. At the time, the decision to give up the twins for adoption was not much of a question. It was a foregone conclusion to deliver the children, and another foregone conclusion on her part to give them up to God's fate, and a welcoming family. The reality that she could not keep them, and does not know them now, has always haunted her. That is my belief and understanding from what I hear, and what I am told. She has been saving people ever since the trying days of her youth, and doing her best for her family, despite herself. She is so loving and committed to doing her best, that she even provides a home for her three younger brothers; angel Fear; angel Loathing; and angel Recrimination. You just cannot write a story about angels as good as the reality Fury lives in; a family so eternally aligned, that four of the angelic core live under one roof.

Spite's three younger brothers are my uncles. My three uncles are unearthly spiritual beings who have each lived lives with one foot wedged firmly in eternal being, and the other foot planted solidly into mortal flesh. If they each had an extra foot, it would probably end up where the sun does not shine. Together my three uncles idealize the mythological three headed dog Cerberus, the Hound of Hades. Forgive me here; I do not really believe there is a three headed dog that guards God's gate to Hades. I do believe that these three beings operate more effectively on a rotating shift, and that nothing gets into or out of Hades, unless it is at God's direction. If my uncle's were the three heads of Cerberus; Cerberus would have long ago fought itself to death, and there would have been an open job posting to serve at that gate.

To be clear; in general, Hades is not for humanity to worry over or understand as s possible reality waiting at the end of mortality. The things that God keeps in Hades are there for good reason; that is God's business. Knowledge of Hades, and understanding of Hades, and maintenance of Hades is left to God, the Supreme Being. I will venture no further into Hades, except to simply remind you that the son of God vanquished Hades long ago, with his Father's help, through their commitment to humanity by way of forgiveness.

You can be relieved that humanity is not bagged like groceries in death; some for Hades and some for heaven; do not spend your life dwelling over a threat of a hateful existence. Salvation means salvation. Every worldly system of belief points straight to the benevolent God; do not be tricked into learning that God is anything but heavenly; do fear God in life when you abuse God in life; plan on embracing God when you pass; He made it clear and simple for good reason. Life is hard enough already without you having to contemplate dying, and being sent to toil in an unpleasant afterlife; leaving behind relations that also now imagine you are drowning forever in your own poor choices. God did not spend a lifetime creating your unique self only to waste you. He does not waste what He creates; take it easy and enjoy life as best you can.

Freedom of worship and practice is included in the truth; practicing with the fear of Hades in your heart is your decision; speak for yourself clearly; God and the son, together with all of heaven, take great pains to remind you to study the good word plainly and simply and with a clear heart free of fear.

Spite is a common emotional event, akin to Hate, but much more manageable. Spite can be a liberating force that actually helps create balance in human existence. Spite cannot lead to death, unlike her big sister Jealousy. Spite is a petty version of hate. Hate is a strong emotion, and a massive consumer of energy. Hate is an unhealthy thing, and can lead to physical ailment; Spite on the other hand may cause some indigestion, and lead to trouble sleeping, but that is about all. A little spite never hurt anyone.

Hate can destroy greatness, and even kill things that would otherwise have remained honest and true. Hate can leave the mightiest of men weak, and begging for relief. Hate can lead men into praying for revenge, and praying for forgiveness in the same breath. Hate is an awful brew of fear, loathing and recrimination; when combined with anger and fury, hate can lead to destruction and chaos. Hate is a bitter thing when it afflicts mankind, but just another tool that helps the world and heaven go round and round. Hate, Spite, Love; they are each the children of emotion, and beloved of God, the Supreme Being.

Such powerful symbols including jealousy, spite, fear, loathing, recrimination, fury, anger, and hate, are some of the things the Lord sent into the world to help signal the change of the epoch. (It seems God Himself does not shy away from showing a little spite now and then.) Study your history well, and understand that the purpose of history is to show God, and to protect the future. This is God's world, believe it or not; it was His decision to send the angels He sent; apparently angel Happy Go Lucky was not included.

The world of human history is the result of His purpose through design and creation that He uses to ensure the future He desires for humanity. Childhood is for growing and learning; adulthood is for knowing and understanding. The past is there to ensure the future is protected. Children fight and can certainly hurt one another; men, though, could easily cause the destruction of even God's great vision for mankind's future. He will not have mankind living in jeopardy of destroying His world that He shepherds so carefully for us.

The weapons of adulthood that man creates are much more dangerous than his childhood toys; man's thoughts are more easily corrupted when one half of the world plays, and the other half starves, and we watch it on the daily news; God did not send the angel Happy, because He needed to send angels of warning.

Angel Spite was well chosen by God for the mission, so that the children of Spite would become who God needed them to become. Spite has led a gentle emotional life, even though she has been confronted with emotional turmoil; she has remained graceful under great stress. Despite the difficult path that destiny provided for her, she has remained calm and steadfast. Her path has been difficult, yet critical for God's mission. Redemption says it always did take a lot to make Spite mad, but after her mother had reached the breaking point, her measures of punishment were spiteful indeed. Her implements of childhood punishment included spatulas and bars of soap; powerful tools to a child, not too frightening for adults.

Angel Spite's burden of learning exists in reality when she consistently chooses to be nice and avoid the pitfalls of a spiteful nature. She endeavors to help those that she could help, and faces reality when there is no help. Angel Spite has leant the helping hand when no one else would. Spite has stepped into the risks presented by obvious trouble in order to make the lives of her family better, even when there was no tolerance given by others, and even when friendship had personally been abandoned. Angel Spite just does not have a spiteful bone in her body.

Angelic learning takes a back seat for angel Spite now; she surpassed the need to demonstrate learning in front of God, who asked so much from one life, and placed so much karma in her way, to create the road she had to travel to bring us to today. Pray to God to deliver peace through the greatness of knowing success in reality. Without popularity, gospel does not deliver magic, but remains merely hocus pocus; through popularity, gospel comes into greatness. Help the family core to see their lives through the eyes of success. Each member of my family was told, one way or the other, they were angels on earth; it may help everything to hear it from you. That is my burden to ask, and to share.

The Queen Mother's message to the archangel is to be ready for delay; to remain calm and maintain patience as the gospel spreads its way into the world. Time is precious, and mankind may be loath to be generous with it. A spiteful attitude on the part of a furious angel on earth will not encourage man's generosity with understanding. A generous nature is helped along when there is plenty of time to allow for the steady growth of understanding. Generosity, understanding, knowledge, and acceptance will only come willingly when niceness and hospitality are maintained, and the greatest of available wisdom is employed. Spite, fear, loathing, and recrimination will not foster the contemplative nature of man, while he considers something as awkward as the modern testament, directed at the entire world and all of belief.

At fifty-three Fury has little time to waste; there is anxiety and loneliness in delay; the potential lack of legacy drives the heart of Fury bananas, adding to the heavy weight on the one set of mortal shoulders responsible for it all. The most difficult part of knowing the truth of the gospel is to accept the passage of time gracefully. Grace is a beautiful and special thing to both give and to receive; embracing the ideal of extraordinary being is to exist within the very moment of what it means to be human, and to offer humanity's truest virtue in the face of the improbable possibility described by Fury. If this gospel lacks grace, and does not add up to truth; explain with your heart what more you need, then by the grace of God it may yet be provided; demonstrating grace in the face of heavenly story is a rare opportunity, and may require men of great wisdom.

Spite's message to the world of man is to avoid a spiteful nature, it's a bad practice. A good practice is to be nice regularly, and enjoy a healthy life filled with niceness, and then nice things will come your way. Remember the golden rule; do unto others as you would have them do unto you; be nice, and read your gospel twice.

SECTION V

Angel Fear

ANGEL FEAR WAS BORN IN 1948, AND IS THE FIFTH MESSENGER belonging within the family core. Angel Fear is the fourth sibling of my father angel Understanding's generation. God decided to send the angel responsible for monitoring eternal and mortal fear into the world of man for this modern mission and story at the start of the second millennium. Fear is a serious thing, suggesting concern, rather than calm.

Who would think that in the year 2016, you would read such a thing as the modern testament claiming to contain the word of God, and that God would send a messenger named Fear into man's world. How can it be that in these times, where everyone above the of age eight apparently has a smart phone, God sends beings like Jealousy, Spite, Fear, Loathing, Recrimination, and Anger; and the chief angel of the mission, claiming to be God's author, would be named Fury. If you think about it carefully, you'll realize it was necessary.

Can a rational mind accept that there is such thing as a heavenly epoch every two-thousand years, and that God celebrates such things as this, and sends special gifts including Fear into the world? Did you anticipate that the Supreme Being would provide a story teller so you could read about His modern history, and know that He has concerns for the future and makes plans? Did you anticipate the arrival of the Archangel of the First Epoch of God; or did you think God had stopped caring enough to show you things you need? Have no fear; God did not forget; yes, He sent fear; not to alarm, only to remind.

God is gracious and shows you He cares when He reminds you of the relevance of fear, so that you embrace His benevolent nature with hope and promise for the future He has in mind; the best advice is to tolerate each other willingly; know that simple truth is the most truth, and that is what the Shepherd planned. When mankind tolerates with respect and an open heart, there will be peace, and the gentleness of love will grow. Fear is a good thing; God sent Fear for good reason; fear keeps us sharp and clever; fear for your love in order to protect respect; fear losing respect so you fear for yourselves; losing respect will cost you your love of hope, and the promise of a future secured in love, rather than in fear of war.

Love, hate; life, death; these things all work together as the means to the end; in the end there is light for everyone, that is the admitted truth of the gospel. Celebrating the light of salvation is the goal of the modern gospel. Yes, Fear is here with us, and will help us understand that God likes a good celebration to honor existence, and to keep us on our toes.

Love Him, praise Him, fear Him; understand He is benevolent and provides ongoing works to demonstrate His forgiving nature.

Suggesting God was done sending His word should create fear in us all; losing His words or discarding His words is plain wrong; ignoring discovery is a bad idea; when He is setting things right you should abandon fear, and understand it took great effort to secure things He intended to remain safe, and embrace these things when He restores His treasure to the light of the world.

Fear has a hard time with God. In his youth, my uncle Fear was headed to the priesthood. When he arrived at seminary school some inconsistent teaching took place that he could not agree with, and would not accept. Since he is burdened with learning everything concerning Fear, he has a tendency to lack fear. Fear's lack of fear is karma's way of directing God's heavenly requirement toward angelic learning, by forcing encounters where fearful decisions have to be made, so that valuable knowledge is gained, and the messenger's value to God and us all, is increased.

My uncle, angel Fear, is pretty much fearless, and will impose on you for as long as your patience permits. He is a traveler and philosopher; he currently visits with relatives, and lives in camp sites. He has a small car, and a small tent. My uncle is a homeless veteran. He served two tours of duty in Vietnam. Angel Fear tells the world there is no God, and that religion is designed to take advantage of lesser minded people.

Fear lives every day anticipating, but not believing, that God will show Himself by striking my uncle directly in the heart with a bolt of lightning from heaven. He and his father, my grandfather, have both prayed mightily to God to send the lightning so that their mortal hearts could know God's presence while they lived. It may be that only the lightning bolt to the heart will allow fearless angel Fear to turn back to heaven and embrace God, and thank Him for His mortal touch albeit though a lightning strike. He will probably require blue skies to be shining, and no thunder clouds to be hanging around, or the lightning strike will seemingly not have been sent by God for him especially, and will only have been sent by accident. Since lightning never strikes twice, let's hope the lightning bolt comes in clear skies; Fear long ago grew impatient waiting for God to show Himself.

When Fear was attending seminary school, the Catholic rules were changed so that the obedient could once again eat meat on Fridays during their sacred day of fasting. The church admitted that eating meat on Fridays would no longer be considered a mortal sin whose transgression earned the violator a place in Hades. This was a great relief to many including butchers.

My uncle, the thinker, wondered about the new situation, and considered salvation from eternal pain for so many sinners. He questioned his instructor the priest, possibly out of concern for others, definitely out of his need to understand the rules that sent people into immortal turmoil.

He asked the priest whether or not the people, who had consumed meat last Friday before the heavenly rule was changed, would still be condemned, or whether they were forgiven as well, and therefore saved from eternal doom.

In front of his seminary class, the instructor waved the question aside. When my uncle persisted, the instructor informed him, under a shaking finger, that if the student persisted any further that he might indeed be sent to eternal ruin himself. This may have been the moment in time when the adult angel Fear no longer feared. Apparently the eternal being in angel Fear, had no fear that the priest had the power to send him to an unpleasant immortal existence. My uncle left seminary school, and followed a different path.

We already know and understand from teaching that the gate to Hades is guarded carefully; no being gets in; no being gets out; Hades is reserved for special reason, and purpose; we defer to God for that, and venture no further into God's business. Forgiveness of mortal sin and heavenly salvation for all is actually a simple reality that God enjoys; Hades is not for the things that God values; Hades purpose is real, and really God's business alone. Ask Him later about Hades; it is a favorite question of His; remember angel Fear and how perceptions can change if God offers to show you Hades and what it holds safe.

There is no thinking more powerful than experiencing a loss of understanding; loss of understanding frees the mind from fear as we desperately seek to understand once again; that freedom from fear is a powerful force creating the ability to think quickly. My uncle has spent his life confronting fear while searching for truth, and thinking about things in order to fill in the missing pieces of a reality he cannot fully grasp, but fears may exist. Karma exists all about his being, leading him on the path of study, thought, and reason; yet karma does not deliver the truth he seeks; his eternal being is so strong, that he cannot determine which foot to trust; the one planted in eternity, or the one standing on God's green earth.

Angel Fear bears the heart of fear into the world to teach us, above all else, to fear God's power over humanity. God will create and direct any life He chooses; He can create and will direct a generation of men if He chooses; He is the shepherd of humanity, and heavenly design and creation remains His domain.

Fear gives us the greatest tool we can use to love and understand God best; respect. Understanding the usefulness of respect provides us the tool to understand that we must fear God more than we love ourselves. God spends the time and energy to teach us out of His benevolence and respect for humanity. He takes the time to create knowledge and understanding out of His desire for continued progress toward Him. He spends His energy designing the works so that purpose is delivered into the world so we can have visible evidence of His being and desire. This is gospel.

Cherish your fear of God, and treat God with respect; God will do the rest, and goodness will grow in heaven, and in man. You should fear each other less; respect each other more; appreciate each other's intellects fully; that is the path to goodness; that is what is necessary for humanity grow in the proper direction.

Remember, it is simple, there are thousands of years ahead of man, getting the basics sorted out amongst yourselves now will allow God to do what he likes best. He likes best to teach Himself to the innocent. He likes for man to maintain the path to goodness, and to Him. Shepherding history, and making things right, does not have to be a repetitive action, where God constantly rearranges mankind's fate, and teaches man lessons over and over.

It is not that difficult to understand the few simple rules; He makes it simple out of necessity. Keep your eye on your own destiny, and your fate will be written as you intend it to be read. Jeopardize the future, and you will have another angel telling you about your real history another time. The history you understand now may not be the history you understand a hundred years from now, since God works in mysterious ways.

Fear not; God created man in His own intellectual image; respect the intellect of God, and then you will respect one another; fear each other's God given intellect, and you will lose respect for one another; lose respect for one another's intellect, and that is where the lines of destruction lie waiting. Shared intellectual reasoning among men along spiritual lines leading to the one God in heaven will keep any world safe and secure, as long as trust and freedom are included in the reasoning. God loves argument for argument's sake; just don't fight over spirituality; argument is healthy and embracing disagreement should be constructive.

My uncle bears much weight upon his broad shoulders. He has learned all of his life. His burden is real. His learning is real. The angelic nature of mortal existence has brought him into a lifetime of direct conflict with karma because he lacks fear of being. His learning is a work in progress.

Twisting the entirety of humanity into belief through The Gospel of Fury: The World of Make Believe requires much use of fear, and some hope for success. Angel Fear teaches Fury, Archangel of the First Epoch of Man, to create the element of fear in the world by inserting doubt and confusion, and by using reality to make mankind question just what it is he thinks he knows and believes about God's goodness, so that the magic of the almighty can be seen, and admitted into the modern world on a universal basis, and in a fresh light.

Admitting that God's apocalyptic justice of the twentieth century is a reality for the world in which we live, is a fearful thing to accept. Contemplating that apocalyptic justice is God's heavenly teaching, and that He desires the world to understand His need for balance, is another step in knowing the fear He is capable of inspiring for the sake of achieving His purpose. Teaching and spreading gospel that the son of God came two thousand years ago for everyone, and without any commitment or requirement, can sound like a lack of respect for tradition and heritage, and cause fear of the potential exposure to unknown heavenly consequences. Yet, these are the things God gave the archangel to give to the world of man to remove doubt and uncertainty, and to remind the world of God's commitment to simplicity and goodness including His being and name. These are just a couple of the situations that may increase man's level of fear, and build respect for the gospel.

The future depends on understanding that the gospel of today is not arbitrary and just for fun. The Supreme Being is sending the gospel now to protect the future, and avoid the potential disasters of religious war and terror, for His own sake and ours. Human beings are free to conduct warfare and to deliver terror, but only in their own name and out of their own desire. Kill yourselves all you want, heaven awaits your soul's arrival in any event; just never again give God and heaven the credit for your own mortal choices.

This is God's mission to earth, it is Fury's mind and fingers mixing up the words; do not be too afraid of Fury's words alone, since Fury may not have yet earned your respect, and without respect, fear is just a fleeting notion. Real fear is a powerful motivator that will affect any man and any group. Gaining your respect out of fear will only work if the fear is based on your true belief in the teaching and knowledge gained through studying and understanding this gospel. Only time will tell if Fear helped.

For the first two thousand years, we may have been alarmed that God would ask a father to sacrifice his child to demonstrate his faith in the good Lord. In modern times, Fury passes on God's teaching which asks you to know that God desired two world wars, along with the assassination of the American president, who is an angel, just so heaven would not feel so slighted with mankind's mortal abuse in God's name. God never needed destruction and war in order to place His being into the heart of man; all God needs is a little opening in the heart, and His openings will not be made with bullets and bombs, and should not have been made with swords and axes.

God's objective for the archangel is to reach all of mankind universally; the information in the gospel is universal, since God is the universal Supreme Being. The archangel was not sent for one race, or one continent, or one religion; the archangel was sent with the simple things God provides to bring it all together in time for the passing of the epoch, and for the future we all need.

Of course the Supreme Being included Fear in the mission; how could He achieve success without reminding man to fear mightily so that He maintains the respect He needs to make the magic of belief real for the modern world.

SECTION VI

Angel Loathing

THE SIXTH ANGEL SURROUNDING FURY FOR THE MISSION OF THE epoch is Loathing, dread of the heavenly angels, and self professed black sheep of the mortal family. Angel Loathing was delivered into the world in 1950. The child and the man have never quite found home in mortal life; the eternal being is too strong, and my uncle prefers himself over humanity. He describes heaven as existing all around him here on earth, and when you see the world through eyes filled with self love, this is especially true. It is admitted, God's paradise on earth is similar to heaven; life on earth can be as good as dreams of heaven, so if you like dreaming about heaven, then you will love the perfection of heaven.

My grandfather hoped his fifth child would turn out to be the golden boy. Blessed with youthful good looks and athletic ability; grandfather planned for the child to grow into a successful sportsman, and bring riches and fame to the family. Alas, if you happen to be the angel Loathing, and are consumed with karma inspired self-love, and are your own golden boy, you cannot hope to fulfill another person's dreams for their pot of gold at the end of their rainbow. There just are not enough two ended rainbows waiting to be found. Grandpa got the short end of that stick.

My uncle speeds through life like a jet airplane. When Loathing came of age and discovered manhood, he also discovered fatherhood. Instead of sports, he found work, and raised his daughter along with his youthful wife. Uncle will tell you he broke his father's heart when he himself became a father, and derailed Grandpa's dreams for the sporting life and riches. The train carrying my grandfather's hopes and dreams had left the station without him, and my ornery uncle willfully became the engineer, yanking long and hard on the train's steam whistle, while grandpa watched his dreams fading away.

My grandfather always felt God near to him in life; he was blessed with an important heart and strong being; that is how his children saw him, that is how his grandchildren held him in awe; he did not know he served the Lord directly; I do not believe he knew he fathered six of God's messengers who would lead to the lightening of a self-professed archangel, and the telling of this story to celebrate our special time. Through his fifties, grandfather stood barrel-chested, tall, and always remained Hollywood handsome. He passed back to the maker 1/19/1991. He never got to witness two of his grandchildren wed one another on their path to fulfilling heavenly destiny in the form of a story designed so carefully as gospel. He would be proud of us, and our children.

When he arrived back at the gates of heaven, Grandpa surely accepted his warm greeting from the watch angels, then undoubtedly slapped his great palm down on one knee and proclaimed, "Well I am surprised, I did not realize it in my lifetime on earth; we were entrusted to deliver a serious level of burden, and I didn't even know it; I am not so shocked." Then he would have twinkled, and said, "I thought I felt like something special all my life." He led a hard life seeking happiness, pay check to pay check; like most of us.

Angel Loathing is one of the three heads of the three headed beast Cerberus that guards the gate of Hades. My entire life has played out in witness to my uncle's unearthly antics. His being is larger than his mortal life can contain; body and mind seemingly splitting at the edges with joy; earth is his heaven with no desire to contemplate any greater purpose. He lives life knowing God personally; which is a good thing, and points to his sense of self-importance. I have told him he is an angel on earth, but I do not know if he heard me. He probably heard me, but understood on his own what he needed to do concerning his own greatness. We all have paths to follow; some paths deliver more eternal presence than is common. Heaven's reach has maintained an uncommon grip on the earthbound angel Loathing. Be cautious if you meet the angel, it may be frightening; there are much more pleasant angels on earth than Loathing.

The three brothers, angel Fear, angel Loathing, and the youngest, angel Recrimination; are beloved of God and blessed in life; albeit with spirituality that is hard to place a finger on. Their lives have been plagued with unease and wandering. Angel Loathing, though, is on a whole other level when it comes to misplaced spirituality. My uncle's spiritual love for himself places the rest of the world, and humanity, in second place. His sister angel Spite, the nicest of souls, provides a home for him. He lives in the lap of luxury atop a great mountain. The good Lord saw fit to have four of my family located together under one roof. Spite, Fear, Loathing, and Recrimination; they all remain alive so far, and no one has yet been badly injured; feelings get stepped on as a matter of routine. My father-in-law lives in bewilderment as he sees that the golden years are not really so golden after all. What can you expect when you live with four angels that are still in the middle of fulfilling God's real time prophecy?

Why does the gospel use symbolism and represent Cerberus, a mythological Greek beast assigned the task of keeping the gates of Hades safe and secure? To remind mankind that our universe, including heaven and Hades are God's domains; God is the shepherd of humanity; mankind is the shepherd of the earth.

Keep life simple; life is full enough pay check to pay check; hunger is real for many. Worry more about helping one another rather than what broken things God keeps under guard in Hades; remember, God does not waste what He creates. He creates things to love; you don't have the power to change that love by the actions of your life time. There is no act on this earth that will remove God's love from you, or change the bond of forgiveness that exists between the Father and the son. Dead human beings and souls carrying lifesavings are not sorted out by those who are good, bad, or indifferent.

God needed to remind us of His love so He sent Fear, Loathing and Recrimination. A three headed dog guarding the gate to Hades is more frightening than angel Gloomy, angel Pouty, and angel Down and Out Sad. Gospel needs to be somewhat exciting since heaven knows modern man's attention is hard to attract, and even harder to maintain. Things man can recognize and understand are included in this work, thanks to His design and creation; simple angel Fury never maintained a simple imagination; if you truly have faith, then believe in our time; know that the completeness of the story included a complete imagination to go along with an existence open to scrutiny now, and for all time. The world He planned for the gospel is a real world.

Fear, Loathing and Recrimination feed off of one another in a powerful cycle of emotional turmoil that could keep any being, conscious or unconscious, occupied in a state of misunderstanding. Similar to a state of dementia that visits some of earth's elderly, the state of misunderstanding is a practical jail for those beings God has not fixed, has no desire to fix, or cannot fix. (This is more detail regarding the domain Hades, but man needs to understand this story is real, though rare.)

There has to be some fire along with much heaven; balance of truth creates balance of power; power of persuasion must offer delight along with fright. Lightened angel Fury has this one life to represent, and leave you with, so you could know the things heaven needed you to have. No thing God presented could be omitted, even when it sounds as if Fury speaks like the Fallen Angel escapee of heaven, telling God's secrets out of spite to show off, attracting attention. There is detail to satisfy a world of great and diverse people who demand much of their stories; providing detail is necessary to maintain the power of persuasion, and increase the success of heavenly argument.

Loathing is woven into the angelic fabric of this blanket of words, designed to guide you wisely along a path between heaven and humanity to create your desire for understanding, and to acknowledge the difficulty you will face growing into acceptance of the modern word. It is not simply that man is loath to change; it is that man is loath to face up to the reality of possibly working together toward simpler adaptation, and figuring out how to admit, or deciding together if any adaptation through admittance is even necessary. These words are harsh today; in time these words will mellow as all of history mellows. On the one hand, I bring the fright of the world's apocalypse, twice; on the other hand I describe the heavenly Father's quest for the delight of grandchildren admitted on earth as they are in heaven. There is balance of persuasive power through balance of knowledge in represented truth; do not loathe these representations because they confound your mind; face your challenge since it is a rare opportunity to admit heavenly truth into a world in motion.

Breaking down human and spiritual barriers within the college of religions to bring ideas into play, will get things done in the end; accepting and admitting requires work; delivering adaptation requires working together, since heaven is reaching out to the whole world. Is there even such a thing as a Global College of Religious Affiliates? Time is short; Fury's dreams are unlimited; don't let loathing contribute to your delays which control my angelic dreams and heaven's purpose.

The men, women, and children all across this paradise of earth live at different levels of success and that relates to their need for God's fresh word. The poor may be loath to pay the price of the gospel, and to invest the time to read it, not sure if its benefit is real, or whether it even applies to them. The poor will wonder if the gospel will deliver them to their next level of happiness; which is all they really care about during life, most of them knowing they are already saved for heaven and truly blessed.

The rich may be loath to review the modern gospel, because it may tax their intellect, and force them to interact with others to question understanding, and that just may be too much extra work for their already successful lives. The learned and powerful may be loath to consider the modern word since it will definitely force them to confront a reality they understand

and support faithfully. The skeptics of the world, who are God's favorites, will simply enjoy the gospel is passing, and accept its reality readily. If Fury did the job correctly, the cynics will be relieved that the skeptics and the faithful have one more thing to keep them occupied. Angel Loathing reminds us, that we loath every aspect of change and even accommodation, especially when tradition and heritage are perceived in jeopardy. This story confounds by admitting all of tradition and heritage as being of God.

Love God, praise God, fear God; do not loath God's effort; you should have anticipated it and admit its position in our modern history.

SECTION VII

Angel Recrimination

THE FINAL CHILD BORN OF HIS GENERATION IS ANGEL RECRIMINATION who came in 1956. He is the sixth member of his family of named angels. Each of these messengers bears the burden of their super power, and each is tasked with heavenly learning. Much of heavenly learning can be completed on the job training in heaven. But life on earth is the most valuable teaching experience of all, and this includes angelic learning. Angel Recrimination is the seventh angel in the family core of twelve, since the core includes my mother, angel Faith.

Angel Recrimination is only seven years older than Fury. Recrimination and Fury played together regularly whenever we visited my dad's parent's house. Recrimination was born when Grandpa was forty-one years old. By then Grandpa had grown accustomed to his routine of running the kids around and maintaining his house the way he anticipated he should have it, though, Grandma never did suffer Grandpa lightly. She kept a special bag reserved for people who misbehaved, and for those who lost her trust. Grandma never minded sharing who of her people had earned their place in her mythical bag. She had no trouble letting you know if you were in the bag, or not. Grandpa also had a special house they called the dog house; and Grandpa regularly occupied that dog house, watched there carefully by grandma until she felt he served his time and earned his penance, and could come out into the light of forgiveness once again. Grandpa could make the sun shine when he wanted to; he could make you know the presence of God, or feel the agony of mortality, depending on his mood.

The family had enough to eat, and Grandpa had plenty to drink. He had friends and frequented several favorite drinking spots. He even maintained his own pin up room across the hallway from where angel Recrimination's childhood bedroom was. When we were growing up, we grandchildren called that special room "Grandpa's Playboy Room". Between the Playboy Room across the hall, and Grandpa's drinking, young Recrimination was exposed to a lot of adult things at a very young age.

My uncle, angel Recrimination, does not place blame for his own decisions and actions on anyone's shoulders than his own. He admits that growing up the youngest of six brothers and sisters, and while his dad was older, and across the hall from the playboy room, may have set him up for a certain adult lifestyle, but he does not accuse anyone other than himself for not becoming everything he could have been. As if being an angel on earth and serving God directly was such a common and easy affair! So, if you accuse him of wasting a gifted life, he will not accuse his parents and family of setting a poor example, nor of neglecting his proper development as the youngest of six children. He has always been the grandchildren's favorite uncle; he has so much to give and so much living to do in our world in motion.

Recrimination is the act of responding to an accuser by accusing him in return. Recrimination has spent his life studying guilt and blame. He has suffered much in life and learned his lesson well. Thank God that the goodness of the Father included a highly educated and experienced staff of angels ready and willing to assist us all in heaven, and in our time on earth. Pray to God; ask Him to send an angel to help you. Bureaucracy is there for a reason; because it works, and because it makes God happy to administer and share heaven's work.

Angel Recrimination's angelic learning was driven along early in his development by his argumentative siblings, including Fear and Loathing.

Imagine the chorus provided by the heads of the dog as they argue amongst themselves over who is braver, uglier, and smarter. I cannot know now, but I imagine the three headed dog is quite a sight to see in the Kingdom of Light. Enjoy your time, plenty of visiting hours are available in heaven, and the lighted kingdom is filled with all the imaginable things of history you want to see, and marvel over. Seeing the light does have its advantages.

My uncle, angel Recrimination, is a wonderful man, but for the largest part of his life he has found much joy in drinking. He grew up under his father's roof understanding that men and families drink to add joy to everything. In those days corn roasts and pig barbecues went hand in hand with coolers filled with ice cold bottled beer. There weren't too many monitors watching which kids were having too many beers either. His youthful demeanor, and a career in the Navy, set the being up for an existence searching for the missing pieces of his soul that always lay too close to his heart to simply pick up and marvel over. Usually it takes the fabric of a family to deliver the clear vision God needs us to see.

Big sister Spite, who is so generous, and just cannot help but save people, opened her doors to her little brother Recrimination, and low and behold the angel shined right up like a brand new penny. The wonder child of our youth, the joy of the party, the angel himself was restored to good health. There is a ship's log of physical ailments to go along with his new life, but for the time being, the grog is in the past. Spite has threatened to cut off his testicles if he drinks again. Maybe Spite is just as nice and she needs to be, and at just the right moments. Big sister does know best.

Recrimination grew up in the family he belonged to as part of the mission God sent him on. His angelic super power is recrimination. The act of recrimination is the act of making an accusation in return for an accusation. He and karma grapple with conditions that force my uncle to gain knowledge regarding responsibility and blame; however, my uncle does not have much of a history of blaming anyone other than himself for his self-destructive behavior.

In their youth the brothers Fear, Loathing, and Recrimination undoubtedly never tired of the game "I know you are, but what am I." So, Recrimination has a leg up on his eternal burden of learning, and may serve the Lord freely now during life. He is young enough to support the mission, provided he is blessed with good health. Oddly, there are not enough angels on earth that know they serve the Lord directly. Lightened angels help to deliver God's joy, and heaven glows in His warmth when He is happy, and the earth experiences elation, albeit a little more difficult to feel than a heavenly hum is to hear.

Angel Recrimination reinforces the archangel's understanding of our family's purpose, and that the mission named The Gemini Star is solidly designed with enough detail to create questions, and bring a fresh sense of God's modern mystery. Fury is not here to accuse man of anything; Fury is only here to present the history of man through the eyes our heavenly Father, to teach the need for heavenly missions, and to bring up a few simple elements to enhance spirituality.

The archangel has no time to banter in a game of recrimination where the world plays "I know you are; but what am I?"; the archangel is giving you everything you need on a silver platter. Your mortal role and responsibility in adulthood is to accept the modern gospel, and to treat it with care; accepting the global gospel is no small task for a wide world filled with diverse nature. You will have to work together, facing the reality of a story that did not start in reality; that is what God expects as He presents His progressive mission.

SECTION VIII

Angel Anger

THE EIGHTH ANGEL IN THE FAMILY CORE, FURY'S BROTHER ANGER, was delivered to the world in 1966. Angel Understanding, together with the angel Faith, delivered the angels Fury and Anger into the world in the 1960's in preparation for what we now suppose is the changing of the first epoch into the start of the second epoch. The first epoch of man's spiritual time is where mankind grows out of childhood and into adulthood.

The responsibilities of adulthood are more complicated as they include accountability, and require more unity than when man was a child. There is no need for too much concern; do not feel threatened; your religious practice and spiritual heritage are intentionally preserved within God's plan for unity of spirit directed toward the Supreme Being, and not away from one another; diversity of worship and religious practice is admirable and needs to be maintained.

It is bold to know, and declare it; God made the decision to send the brothers Fury and Anger into the world; He did not send Happy and Glad. Man has not always been so polite and correct during his childhood, often using God's name in vain. The forgiveness required of childhood was never unanticipated; every world exists along a similar path; every world receives God's touch so that the rightness of the path is maintained.

Imagine that there are many worlds for God to shepherd. Imagine each of those worlds receiving His guidance, and teaching of His desire for each world to know His ongoing love and care, just as a father loves to maintain His family in joy and friendship. Imagine the great benefit in knowing and understanding the benevolence of touch in the modern digital world of today; then understand God's singular desire to remove His name and being from man's potential for warfare and terror. Consider all the years of time and generational effort God and heaven invested in planning for this mission and the modern gospel, just to spell out His needs and plans for mankind's continuity, including progress toward God and heaven. Consider then the ideal of a pure gospel, containing all the things man and heaven need to keep the path clear for progress, and then admit the gospel; shape existence through the gospel, and shape the heavenly lives that deliver the gospel; bridge the lives He planned for; deliver the heavenly existence He desires.

Angel Anger is the calmest of fathers, the calmest of brothers, and the best of friends; to make angel Anger angry takes a lot of effort. Anger is an ancient emotion, and has visited the world on many occasions during many events; Anger must be special, since he is such a routine visitor. The earth and man have shared God's anger often; and the earth and man have contributed to God's anger many times, many more times than God is willing to count or let go; a perfect reason for a perfect time for God to send His modern gospel filled with redemption.

In adulthood, the world maintains accountability and responsibility with heaven and God as it relates to how we have treated one another over history. Redemption is an ongoing process involving the care of historic record and the reconciliation of the record; if we do not study the past, we are doomed to repeat it. History is not just for the young in school; history is for teaching and admonishing and even argument; cost is cost, understanding cost and benefit is a higher order of effort; intellect and reason will evolve within man so that man sees more benefit for humanity than commerce alone. Balancing the books of history is a role for religion and spirituality, designed to bring heaven and earth closer together, and to bring the college of understanding to the forefront of human community and effort; do not leave the understanding judgment provides in the shadows, in the wings.

Understand that you are behind in your collective efforts to keep the books of mortal justice in balance. Ignoring past transgressions, and attempting to allow time to bury wrongs, is not the wisest approach; God knows what lies in the hearts of men, and God carries that burden in His heart; communities have suffered in His name, and while He can right those wrongs in heaven plainly, mortal righting of wrongs through forgiveness and redemption helps heavenly bureaucracy. Resources are resources; why not get things done on earth rather than in heaven; if the earth can get a head start on heavenly work, it would be the wisest use of resources and a good approach. In other words, bury anger on earth, rather than bringing your anger with you to heaven.

Great religious power does not always provide for great religious effort or work. The powerful and the mighty include the rich and well to do; the rich just have too much to do with their time to consider that there may be necessary wrongs that need to be righted, and that resources are scarce for such good works as forgiveness among men while they still live. God gave apocalyptic forgiveness to mankind for transgressions against His name. You still owe it to yourselves to admit to atrocities among yourselves, and to say you are sorry for the historic misdeeds of religious zealotry, and for not doing enough to prevent persecution and suffering in the modern world. These are the things to study so that history does not repeat itself.

Angel anger is an ancient emotion angel, and has much learning in his heart already. His burden of learning is not so much a mortal burden as it is an eternal weight. Anger has much to manage in the Kingdom of Heaven; Anger has sacrificed a day of heavenly time and work to be a part of this mission; when God asks for your participation there is not much choice but to say yes and there is a little wiggle room; He is a kind God. Be kind to Anger while my bother visits the world of man; keep some of your anger to yourself while he lives. He is a kind man, and I do not ever remember seeing him suffer.

Anger is one of the industrious of the heavenly domains. Yes, there are eruptions of anger in heaven as well as on earth. Do not pretend that the Kingdom of Light is all wonder and glory. The bureaucracy of heaven was engineered effectively to enhance equality within eternal existence while we move about at the speed of light; heaven also lends its eternal power of being to the world of time on earth, to help with your prayers and your path.

Tonight, turn on the news and pay attention to the stories filling the television screen that display how often mankind shares his anger and frustration. There is enough mortal violence passed among human beings so that any visitor to earth would understand the complexity of the human condition. Thank the Lord for forgiveness on earth, and in heaven. Thank the son for his unconditional love, and for the bond he maintains with his Father, so that we are all forgiven at judgment. Thank each other for balancing love and hate, and for carrying the weight we call human existence. Don't share more anger than is necessary; anger can kill.

Never forget to seek and pay attention to the stories where mankind shares its love with one another. Do not be sickened with humaniy's willingness to display and demonstrate anger on a regular basis; what we know to be inflammatory news seems to gain the majority of the limelight; man's ability to display love, kindness, and goodness occur in most moments of every second of every mortal day; putting out the flames does not attract as much attention as the fire does; be blessed in knowing we are mostly good folks dedicated to keeping the fires under control. After all, we are good enough, and we will survive far into the future.

Anger provides his big brother Fury with simple knowledge and patient understanding. Be prepared for a rash response to a story filled with apocalyptic events and anti-Christ symbolism that at first glance may seem like grandstanding.

There are plenty of one line, one thought, one message items in this gospel that can be taken out of context, in an attempt to cause an inflammatory response intended to provoke rejection of God's modern word, and Fury's testament. Rash negative response may delay and confuse the gospel's good intent, and confound the archangel's desire to pursue God's greater goals for the angels on earth. Then again, a hot press can encourage a viral response, and a trending situation that would increase the reach of the gospel, but also create exposure. Rejecting the testament, and painting the gospel in irony will confound the messenger only temporarily; words that are preserved for history will still yield the result heaven intends; shaping the story into your existence is the desirable path, and just makes good sense. Consider the gospel and take your time, but not too much time.

The Gospel of Fury is real time prophecy in 2016, and there is a watch and see element of waiting that contains very real consequences and potential outcomes; destiny is close at hand, but still allows for many potential paths; the future lies beyond our lives, and history will play witness to how epoch man handled this little mission called The Gemini Star.

Anger provides the world with a good look at itself, but not for the most part; for the most part we are good, especially with one another; groups, not so much. The larger part of the world only requires a little reassurance that God is here, and that He is always able to provide what He wants the world to know and embrace. God probably sent His angel Anger to increase worry, fear and concern, so that the world knows God's word is serious, and that He carefully takes the trouble to prepare it and send it, and makes it apparent and real through stars of creation to show this as His true story for the epoch.

Angel Anger is indeed my immortal brother; angel Anger and angel Fury are ancient beings created long ago to serve heaven, and God. Angels long ago began their assignments assisting the heavenly Father in the daily routine that He enables. He is the task master of the universe, and takes His pleasure in designing and administering His universe however He sees fit.

We won't spend more time discussing God's anger, or my brother the blessed angel Anger; mankind maintains enough anger on his own without having to be reminded of it further. Just be cautious and remember, Anger is in the world visiting; he is not in heaven today monitoring anger in the world; be careful. A heavenly day is roughly seventy-five earth years, one average lifetime; angel Anger still has more than half a life to live, so be good, keep your anger inside yourself, and let it fester in your own heart where it belongs, rather than letting it out where it can hurt or even kill another human being. Keeping anger in your heart will eventually allow it to mellow from hate into love; that is what it means to be human, and to belong to eternity. Letting your anger out through poor decisions while creating undesirable actions is the result of a lack of love and true understanding of goodness; spread the goodness, spread the word, spread love, decrease the level of disaster. Give Anger a break; he has enough to do already.

SECTION IX

Angel Redemption

ANGEL REDEMPTION IS THE NINTH ANGEL OF THE MISSION. SHE IS a Gemini born on May 29, 1968. She is the first named angel of the close core of messengers belonging to The Gemini Star mission. This mission is designed cleverly by God, and it is intelligently delivered into the world through His power over creation. This mission comes to the world at the passing of the First Epoch of Humanity into the Second Epoch of Humanity to describe the past, and to shape the future. This mission delivers promise, and offers hope.

There are facts in the story presented as shining stars that are each verifiable, and the reality of the inspirational writing is self-evident, even though it is far fetched. You will determine the value of this gospel, and decide whether its expression of truth creates immediate concern, or whether saving the truth for the world of tomorrow is more suitable; acting proactively and collectively in order to maximize God's gift of opportunity is a wise conclusion, and a monumental task. Angels on earth will live and die like every human being; however, their remains may not be as interesting as the true stories of their lives. Believing in them today may help them to leave a little more of their story behind. Burying the truth with them would be unwise, since this is God's truth and heaven sent. These things that are brought, are brought purposefully, and are designed not to fail or end up missing.

Identifying and vetting the facts that are heaven's stars is important since the message of the gospel is real time, and needs to be judged relative to the probability that <u>The Gospel of Fury</u> is truth from heaven, and that God, the Supreme Being, intended epoch man to embrace the words in real time in order to clear a path to perceived destiny. Scholarly review that examines the evidence of the presented facts, and the description of God's truth and worldly desire, should be executed with the care and respect that rare words warrant. If you already have plenty of modern gospels, accept my apologies for appearing inappropriate. My understanding is this is exactly on time and needed, even if unexpected.

The close core of angel's on earth are the four children of angel Spite, which include angel Redemption, angel Peace, angel Love and angel Doubt. These four brothers and sisters, possessed with special nature or character, helped lighten angel Fury in 2014, so that the story became clear, and the gospel would be written. Without a complete cast of angels and character, the truth may not have been visible, and the mission may not have had the depth necessary to deliver the word of God to a modern audience.

I have spent my life searching for possibility, so the special identities of the eight older family members has become obvious, including: angel Jealousy, angel Understanding, angel Faith, angel Spite, angel Fear, angel Loathing, angel Recrimination, and my brother angel Anger.

All together it took twelve messengers, each with specific God given character, and what Fury calls super power, to reveal the reality of an intelligently designed mission that was created out of intent to serve heaven's purpose. The mission is sent at this time to show man the things he needs from the past, and to ensure the future the shepherd seeks. No big deal; just write interesting angelic testimony, and remain convincing, so that there is an increasing popular awareness of the need for global harmony toward God, by reminding man of His desire for unique and special beings. Diversity in man's worship keeps the world of mankind interesting to God, and the diversity of human tradition and heritage provides heaven with the variety of beings that make heaven a rich and happy place. God does not need cookie cutter on earth or in heaven.

Love God, praise God, fear God; share His love of individual character and spiritual diversity.

The Gospel of Fury including The Gemini Star and The World of Make Believe, along with the Archangel propounding the words, admit that all of the children of humanity belong with God and heaven in forgiveness and in salvation, by admitting that the son and the Father commit to each other to provide these things freely through their own heavenly bond, called the Holy Grail in this gospel.

Every single human soul becomes forgiven following judgment day in heaven. Your soul is granted the freedom of the lighted kingdom in eternity after judgment. Get ready to ride the light; it is coming for you. This is the original promise maintained between Father and son.

Judgment is real, and personal. You can be held in judgment for as long as any offended party chooses to hold you in judgment, and remains occupied with you in judgment. Since heaven is waiting though, individual personal forgiveness more likely than not seems like a good alternative; redemption is reached following forgiveness, and your judgment is concluded, and you are a free soul complete with being. Being is the completion of judgment; being is the soul and the life savings together; life savings are gathered in the world as we know it; a complete heavenly being includes a soul, along with plenty of healthy life savings; unhealthy life savings are yours to maintain when needed, and can be a good thing, even though it sounds odd. Heaven does contain some odd things. What you keep in your life savings just depends on what matters to you most; what matters to you most is what you will keep; it's your being to take care of, and to share, if you want.

Justice in heaven is not unlike justice on earth; thanks to the agreement between God and His son, the outcome is known. Forgiveness is just a matter of time, which can occasionally seem like an eternity. Be good; protect your life savings and ensure a swift judgment day; then heaven is yours to explore.

Redemption during mortal life is more complicated than the rubber stamp process in heaven. In heaven, as soon as everybody agrees that enough time has been spent in judgment, then it ends, and heaven begins. Heavenly judgment is not a light matter though, judgment does matter, and the process is closely monitored by the angel Redemption, who is Forgiveness. Like with every bureaucratic process, there are good days and bad days. There are some mortals who leave such trails of sadness behind them that judgment seems to last forever. Some judgment days can consume so much time and energy, that they sound and appear similar to existence in Hades; judgment day is plainly different than being kept in Hades, locked away safely and under control; judgment should not be confused or compared with an eternal damnation.

Spite's twin Gemini daughters born May 26, 1966 are not directly known to Fury at this time, and so as of yet are unnamed angels; not part of the family core of twelve. The twins, together with their brother Peace, born on May 26, 1969, represent the symbolic Gemini Star which launched angel Fury on his writing assignment, representing the paltry messenger of God as he purports to exist. The brilliant Gemini Star which signals our heavenly arrival, exists between the twin girls together with the son Peace, and remains forever; please be careful, and take care of it; it took a lot of mortal time and careful heavenly planning to bring it this far.

The twelve Angels of Common Nature described in Part Two are real, and are wrapped into the life of the archangel. These twelve angels that surround the archangel represent the weight of the enterprise. These ideals are profound, though not more so than the human lives themselves, or the reality of the mission. The significance of each of the twelve characters is embraced by Fury with noble intent, but they exist by God's design and were created in order to be discovered, and then be delivered to the world to fulfill specific intent and purpose.

Fury's ability to interpret the Supreme Being's intent and purpose is a gift you can trust and have faith in; or you can question the presentation, and remain a skeptic that Fury was gifted at all; yet here is the story, and the mission. The value of skepticism is great; the value of sarcasm is little. Healthy skepticism will get you through the gates of heaven without any problems, and will maintain your soul together with your life savings; random sarcasm will leave gaps in your being, and create a thoughtless existence since sarcasm is baseless.

If you have lived at the center of the eye of eternity, or witness the eye of eternity at work knowingly, you understand the subtle quality of gifts from heaven. There are vast amounts of repetitive eternal movement of small events needed for a mortal to remain convinced that the path they are on is just, and that it is the path the Lord intends. Doubt is real, and from day to day, it is normal to feel confident and whole, and it is normal to feel less confident and to worry. Some days we may wonder where our spirits are spending time, since we may feel like we are beside ourselves, or even missing; some days the balance of our existence can exist in eternity; the power of eternal being can come and go; that's the reality of eternal presence in mortal life.

Feeling eternal presence and witnessing eternal intuition are real, and is witnessed by each of us mortals, when we feel our eternal self scratching our mortal imagination so often, that seemingly random innocuous events become noticeable repetitive events, to the point that it makes you wonder. Little quirks in your day that seem out of place or repetitive just may cause you to wonder what's up with that. It is hard to grasp eternal being while you are involved in mortal life. Life already involves too much worry to create much desire to worry about what lies beyond the shadows. When you have randomly looked at your clock at exactly 11:33 so many times that it seems uncanny, give your eternal self a smile, and say thanks, "Thank you, eternal me, for letting me know everything is okay, and we together are real enough to believe."

God and heaven may be mysterious, but a little less so following The Gospel of Fury. This modern testimony ensures man is informed of

God's desire to clear man's collective conscience at the changing of the epoch. This transition from two-thousand years of childhood into the next two-thousand years of adulthood requires the resumption of balance between heaven and earth. It has been long enough now that the weight of mankind's periods of religious and spiritual transgression have remained a weight on the shoulders of God and heaven. There has been enough time spent, while heaven has remained silent waiting for it's absolution from mankind's own destruction, murder, and crime, committed through acts of religious zealotry in the cause of spreading belief. God only needs open hearts; God does not need swords and bullets; God never needed swords and bullets to work His way into the hearts of men and into the world of man with knowledge of His eternal goodness. He is the shepherd of humanity; He does not need mankind to enforce His will through crimes against humanity; His goodness is questioned enough personally, without also having to defend His goodness while man spreads destruction in His name, and in the name of His many beloved religions.

Mankind's warlike transgressions in the name of God actually belong to man; God has no reason to cause persecution and suffering; man can maintain that responsibility on his own shoulders now that man has reached adulthood. If God wants credit for disaster, He will send a messenger to tell you about it, so He can achieve the results He intends.

The physical symbol of the Gemini Star is made by drawing a cross, similar to that wooden cross which bore the weight of the son's body, next to God's sword of justice rising from the earth. These two symbols, the Christian cross and the rising sword of God, when interlocked closely, create the Gemini Star which is the symbolism used for the modern testament. The completeness of the gospel, and God's story, includes the use of symbolism so that the gospel is complete. Because the son of God lived a short life, he did not get much opportunity to create his own set of spiritual practices, nor to leave much written testimony of his own. Following the son's passing, Brother Paul continued carrying the original mission forward into the world which embraces the message just a little narrowly, and with a perceived requirement of conversion. The son's message of eternal salvation along with forgiveness of mortal sin is simple, and was originally intended for the entire world; his message and promise was provided freely without conditions. All of spiritual practice is divine as long as we do not limit the lives of others; God and heaven will deliver the promise; there is no leap of faith required. The modern magic of God that there is plenty of space in the world for distinction between various forms of worship and spiritual practice.

It is necessary to include the symbolism of The Gemini Star, including all the instruction within the written gospel; God inspired the knowledge, and it is not up to Fury, the Being at the Heart of the Sun, to leave anything out of the story. The Father is providing as much inspiration and knowledge as this brief story can contain, so that there is weight behind the truth, and some doubt is removed from the modern world through the magic of His real touch.

Of all the freedoms afforded the earthly world, you can count most on the freedom God gives to believe in the way that helps you to believe the most. Life includes suffering enough without religious dogma adding weight to your shoulders. The Supreme Being, who is the one God of the universe, the one God of eternity and of all time, only asks you to be prepared for heaven; for heaven's sake, do not be so unprepared as to arrive at the gates of heaven oblivious. It is the oblivious soul that may suffer shock. A shocked soul loses track of its being, and its life savings, and may fall apart. Be prepared, even be skeptical, and just don't be oblivious. God won't tolerate long waiting lines at the gates of heaven while busy angels reassemble broken souls. Your soul will be put back together if it does fall apart; but it does take up valuable time and effort, while others wait in line for your being to be gathered up and put back together.

All souls are saved; God does not waste what He creates.

The definition of redemption is that it needs action to deliver results. Redemption is the act of saving or being saved from sin, error, or evil. Redemption is the act of making something better or more acceptable.

It is historically significant that you understand and accept that the modern gospel allows humanity's forgiveness for war and terror using God's name during the first two-thousand years of recorded time, and that it remains as necessary knowledge in order to successfully deliver heavenly balance through the process of redemption.

Admitting that the apocalyptic era begins on January 22, 1901, the day Queen Victoria passed back to God, and that the apocalyptic era ended November 22, 1963, the day President Jack Kennedy was assassinated, remains relevant to redemptive closure by receiving God's judgment and accepting His forgiveness. Mankind's redemption and forgiveness and the restoration of balance between heaven and earth are enabled by intent and design at the passing of the first epoch into the beginning of the second epoch. As shocking as it may sound, the Father, our good Lord, did bring the apocalyptic knowledge through this mission to openly share with humanity; this is gospel. The magnitude of global forgiveness, and it's relevance to the Father, should not be treated with cynicism. Mankind bore the brunt of the hostilities; thank God the apocalyptic hammers are far enough in the past now that memories are not so fresh; heavens gates stayed busy enough, and passed the mighty test God placed on us all.

Angel Redemption is a complicated person. Her role in life is to study man and humanity. She is present at judgment in heaven, and knowledgeable concerning the things that concern us all as human beings, and returning souls. Redemption studies, with curiosity, all the things that we live with, and the things we bring with us in our life savings when we pass. She is an administrator and wise counselor, and will help you get through your own day of judgment; hopefully you will not spend much time with her in heaven. There is much joy to be had in the Kingdom of Light; judgment may be heaven's great sporting event, but it is not the only thing heaven provides for; time spent in judgment keeps you occupied, and out of the light of heaven.

Angel Redemption's message for the archangel is to encourage Fury to remind mankind that redemption is an action or event. Ignoring gospel does not help to complete the process of redemption. You can study the gospel long after the angels pass back to God; however, there is much potential for life, and angels do have hopes and dreams of heavenly purpose. There is much learning to do, there is much more mission to contemplate; get off the couch, and spread the gospel.

SECTION X

Angel Peace

THE HEART OF PEACE WAS BORN INTO THE WORLD ON MAY 26, 1969. The angel on earth, who is my cousin, is the tenth angel in the family core, and is a member of the close core directly responsible for enabling the archangel to see God's modern mission for the first epoch. Peace was delivered by design through creation intelligently exactly three years to the day after his Gemini twin sisters were born May 26, 1966. These dates of birth are verifiable facts, and tie God's stars of design and creation into the lives of the angels as anchors into the reality of the world of mankind. Real evidence of purpose is provided for the earthly mission to help ease skepticism, and to help prevent cynicism. You don't just have to take the gospel on faith when God adds His power to demonstrate His intelligent capabilities.

Man's challenge today is to begin the journey toward eternal peace through recognition; to know God's will is for man to accept his judgment as it has been explained through this gospel; to embrace an understanding of the gospel as it is offered, and indeed needed, by mankind; to admit that heaven in eternity, along with earth in time, will then exist in balance, and reflect man's attainment of adulthood and responsibility, to complete the redemptive event of the global epoch.

Love Him, praise Him, fear Him; do not imagine He will leave Peace out of the modern mission.

The Gemini Star exists as a two dimensional symbol containing the cross of the son, together with the redemptive rising sword of God, as well as the ideal of a signaling star created by the coincidence of Gemini twins born on the same day of the year as their younger brother 5/26 only three years apart.

Within the reality of time, the greater hopes for the mission can expand with the popularity of the written gospel when it is received by the modern world. The scope of real time prophecy will evolve over the next several years delivering increasing purpose while we live, and ensure that the long term goals of the written words are understood, and that they remain intact for the future. The ideal of the journey toward eternal peace is preserved whenever mankind's respect for God wins out in the end, which it inevitably does.

Love Him, praise Him, fear Him; do not waste time wondering if God failed when He created the design for the archangel. God gifted all things to the one life of the archangel to ensure that the modern word would not be overlooked, and become wasted. The claims of Fury are written by design, and intended to provide drama, and attract the attention necessary to encourage discovery, demand verification, and provide for admittance.

In January 2015, angel Spite admitted and reminded nephew and son-in-law Fury that she had given birth to twin Gemini daughters on May 26, 1966. She also reminded Fury that her son, angel Peace had been born the same day May 26, 1969, three years to the day following the twin's birth. That coincidence of Gemini birthdates may seem like just an interesting fact to a casual observer, but for angel Fury it was a signaling star, and the final key to demonstrate God's mystery. Fury's knowledge and understanding of God's intent became robust, and the Gemini Star did launch the writing of the first story, The Gospel of Fury: The Gemini Star, which was available on line in 2015.

Our modern presentation of miracles is in the form of coincidences that exist across the life of the family of angels on earth, and directly influence the author I. B. Fury, and enable the fulfillment of his role as the presenter of the modern gospel. This story differs from creation's original Adam and Eve, but only in the details. Creation has always existed as the domain of God, the Supreme Being, and when He wants to design incredible things, He shall. God's Rainbow of Creation within the Kingdom of Light is a great wonder of the universe, yours now to understand and know through faith, together with signaling stars as they are presented through the real life of Fury; then once again as you pass through the gates of heaven and the rainbow. (I am sure the Rainbow of Creation is a popular attraction in heaven.)

Adam and Eve as the parents of humanity, and the creation of the universe in seven days can challenge modern mankind, and create skepticism when the holy words are treated literally. Your belief and faith are protected in liberty and freedom according to this gospel; it was never this gospel's purpose to change anyone's system of worship anywhere on this planet, or in heaven when you arrive; diversity in heaven is as important there as it is on earth. In adulthood, man needs additional well reasoned insight into His existence through science, in order to help man understand that we are created out of the intellectual image of God for good cause; God could not easily reason with us if our existence were far different from His own. God is clearly and simply reasoning with us now to make us understand the future of armed conflict will not include armed conflict in the name of God, and that is a fundamental purpose of the gospel of the epoch. Don't be surprised; the Earth is not the only world to think it needed to fight over God; God just won't have it here, or in any world, for very long; fight over God in childhood, and admit forgiveness; no longer fight over God in adulthood; do not pretend God needed slaughter or terror to share belief.

God could not easily provide miracles if He were to rely on the parting of oceans, manna from heaven, commandments delivered on stone tablets, or gospel that was sent during an earlier time for a different witness. The rules of reality are valid, and while God and nature work hand in hand, miracles are miracles, large and small. Mankind will continue to evolve, and so may the nature of the stories God sends. This story is for today, but also prepares His word for tomorrow.

God provides the miracles for the modern story, including the Gemini Star, which is our bright heavenly key, and is the anchor that provided simple Fury the path to present the truth of gospel to be delivered to man for God and family.

Angel Peace belongs on this mission, but struggles through his mortal life. On a bad day, he could be so restless and perplexed by life that when you plainly show him a white star and claim it to be a white star; he will call you a liar, and claim that the star is indeed black. The angel is faced with a life confounded by a troubling karma that brings confusion and disbelief. The mortal being grapples against peace of mind in order to fulfill his God given duty to learn all things regarding his super power which is peace.

Angel Peace is a powerful angelic being, responsible for important things in the management of heaven and earth. God and Peace work closely together each heavenly day, maintaining the peace as God desires and hopes for. You yourself may have prayed to God for peace on earth, and you may have prayed to the angel for peace for yourself; either way, peace on earth is not always so easy to find, and not so easy for God to provide; peacefulness is a higher order personal ambition. Mankind maintains free will, and is the shepherd of the earth; God is the shepherd of humanity; God and man are confounded when there is no peace on earth; thank God there is always peace in heaven.

Heavenly peace is assured at the speed of light through heaven's bureaucracy, administered by God. It is true, the Kingdom of Light is not always peaceful; thankfully there is a supporting cast of angels to assist us heavenly beings with equality so heaven functions smoothly; God won't have it any other way; it just makes sense. Heaven is much like life; but being in heaven is a faster thing, and peace is more readily available; the light shines on solutions when peace is the mandated objective rather than a bargaining chip used as a means to another end; face the truth and you will find the avenue to peace when it is your objective. Experiencing a lack of peace is much more likely within the domain of the real world; the reality of peace in heaven is something you can wait for and expect, when you finally pass away.

Love Him, praise Him, fear Him; thank Him for peace in heaven; understand He knows there is a lack of peace in the world; know that peace comes when the poor are happy and fed; happiness has always come when equality is delivered and enforced through the rule of law. Obey the modern commandment to prevent persecution and suffering, then all will be well and peace will reign supreme, and God will work His way into every life.

The poor are the key to peace; the poor have more power in the world than they maintain; use care and ensure there is peace, or the poor may discover the true power of disgruntlement. The rich and the poor together make the world a happy place; God likes peace, because searching for Him is more fun on a full belly.

SECTION XI

Angel Love

LOVE IS THE REASON THERE IS A GOSPEL. THERE IS CLEVERNESS IN heaven just as there is in the world. The Lord is not at all above using a clever plan to ensure the modern gospel is delivered as He intends. He designed and sent the mission including twelve supporting angels, into one family to cause one angel at the center to see patterns and recognize purpose.

I have been looking for patterns all of my life; even though the patterns I recognize are unusual, and represent the footsteps of angels living along predetermined paths that were cleverly created by God; here and now I have recognized the patterns.

He designed Love, and included her to encourage the gospel through the clever use of desire and passion; desire and passion are not unknown to God; do not be embarrassed or shy; desire and passion are well known to God and heaven, and well known as well in the hearts of men, and that's the reality of it.

Love is His most powerful tool to encourage man to follow the direction He intends. To omit love, desire and passion from spirituality is to deny the reality at the heart of humanity, and the image He created. There is no reason, or any sense, in denying the reality of the heart of man. As the shepherd of humanity, God is shepherd of religion and spirituality; to omit love, desire, and passion from spiritual practice and religious dogma, is to attempt to limit the shepherd and His reach; limiting God is a foolish attempt, at best.

God is simply reaching into the real world now to remind us that heaven will not be denied any part of human reality. This is not the story of man's path to God; this is the gospel of God reaching into the world of man to make things clear.

As far as I know, angels are rare, and must therefore be special beings; this gospel then is a rare and special thing too, and demonstrates the reality of God's mission, and His messengers.

Leadership and love exist hand in hand; leadership without love has no heart; heartless leadership cannot deliver the shepherd the future He requires. Be kind to yourselves, and be kind to God; admit desire, passion, love and understanding into spiritual existence; teach one another the importance of the entire human image; after all, we are created in His image, so be honest with yourselves.

We are in the second epoch of humanity now and man is adult; there are two-thousand years ahead for man and heaven together; denying God His path into the future of leadership through creation is to deny Him some of His potential for the future. God would and will choose the very best and brightest for the leadership of His spirituality and global religion. Ensuring the future we all want and He desires, necessitates maintaining God's rights to the future of spiritual leadership through creation; denying spiritual leadership the right to have family and love with desire and passion, is to decrease the depth and dimensionality of leadership's ability to know and help his brothers and sisters while they live their lives. Cutting off God's access to the genetic path He may want for the future makes no sense, and places disadvantage at His feet. Love your family and friends; raise a family while you can; loving God and knowing God is the easier thing, but not the only thing He needs from leadership.

The Lord demonstrated His Rainbow of Creation so Fury can know that the lives for Fury and Love were taken from the same spot within His rainbow of tools; that we would exist as life twins for the purpose of the mission. In our case, we exist as Gemini life twins with Fury born 6/3/1963, and Love born 6/21/1975. For reasons that serve purpose we exist as Gemini life twins, even though we are born twelve years apart. Together our lives were cut from the same spot in the Rainbow of Creation; that original miracle was passed to Fury, and that miracle created The Gemini Star. That was the first big secret, and I could not wait to tell the world; cleverly and by design the gospel continued to grow, and now the original big secret sounds like a fairy tale.

Love the Father, praise the Father, fear the Father; when He provides a miracle, accept the miracle, and share the miracle as He intends; don't hide the truth He provides.

Angel Love was born in 1975, and Fury was born in 1963; together we are born in the Chinese year of the Rabbit and the coincidence adds an element of spiritual truth by supplying detail for the story; thank God for providing signs from creation to back up mortal notion of ideal. Rabbits are the luckiest of the symbols in the Chinese Zodiac, after all.

Love and Fury are alike in many ways, and very different in many others. Love and fury are emotions, and the angels are members of the family of emotion angels. Emotion angels are tasked with guiding man and heaven in understanding mystery and confusion surrounding feelings. Angels also encourage decisions that create activity that can result in steps along a path that inevitably leads people and being into any direction karma intends. Angels are akin to karma; both being members within God's supporting cast of reality. Karma is a complicated thing best summed up in a single word. All you need to do is allow karma to gently guide you along the complicated path of life, and you will get to where you need to be in the grand scheme of things. This story is not the story to explain the world of God's spiritual reality; this is the story letting you know He intended for a world of spirituality.

The beginning of the season of the Gemini is May 22nd, and the last day a person can be born a Gemini in any given year is June 21st.

Angel Love was delivered into the world on June 21, 1975. Angel Love is a powerful servant of God; she is a master administrator tasked with managing the busiest of all the heavenly domains. The number of domains in heaven that support being is only limited by possibility, and anything is possible when it comes to God's good grace. Love touches every human being during life, and in heaven, in a never-ending variety of ways and possibility. Love is endless, and the angel is timeless; in the grand scheme of existence, Love is critical.

Love the Lord, praise the Lord, fear the Lord; know the energy you gain through knowing love closely; explore the energy found in love while knowing life matters for eternity.

Each of us feels and acknowledges love throughout our lifetimes, and we never stop searching for our share of it, as it is central to the soul and life savings. Reaching out and creating love, and then maintaining love in our lives, is probably mankind's strongest desire and need.

Love and passion working together create the most powerful driving force known in reality; the true potential of a human being is realized when love and passion are joined in a direction to create results that can be truly wonderful, or truly terrible. Love and passion can be used for great good; unfortunately the combination of these same powerful forces can also deliver great destruction.

Our own eyes admit our delight with love whenever we meet people with a smile; even though it may be casual, and exist for just a brief moment; the power of love is great even in passing, when we share our smile and represent ourselves with our best look for a stranger.

June 21st is usually the first day of summer in most years. Summer is often considered the season of love in poetry and in stories, possibly due to the slow sultry nights we like to imagine as desirable; I just think summer is hot, and something to survive.

Angel Love is tasked in life with an angelic level of learning that most people cannot comprehend; love can be beautiful and love can be awful; love can create and love can destroy. Imagine traveling to Earth knowing you are about to experience an entire mortal life facing every possible circumstance relating to the set of complex emotional feelings and responses categorized as love; the possibilities are endless, and the work will never end; she will be a tired angel at the end of this life.

Love matters from our first breath to our last breath; when humanity focuses on the importance of love, then we will have reached our destiny. Love and caring for one another is a really big deal; bigger than commerce, but love is treated relative to commerce, for the time being. Discovering the angel herself on this mission is a really big deal, and points to the reality of God's desire for success; guess He could not really have left Love out of the changing of the epoch, since you cannot get from childhood to adulthood without love, and a lot of tolerance.

All the good of love; all the bad of love; all of the unfortunate things and the great things of love find their way to the angel Love by way of karma's influence on life. God has sent the most powerful angel into the world at the epoch; the most powerful angel also happens to face a powerful test of learning while she lives.

Mystery can remain mystery even when you have a key; fear God, praise God, love God; if you don't know your best friend, life may remain a mystery. Love and God are together in heaven during almost every moment; heavenly moments are practical moments, and a lot gets done in a brief moment. In life in 2016, Love is still searching for her understanding of God, and willfully overlooks what is right in front of her. Her spirituality and God's magic are a heavy burden on her; God will one day provide her a walking stick to help her get through her own desert quickly. She has much to provide the world, and heaven in return.

Angel Love turned forty-one in 2016, and her experience and struggle with love is already broad; she could fill a novel with her knowledge. She is still a young woman, and capable of much goodness. She is currently not present in the Kingdom of Heaven since she is serving God on a mission to earth. God included the most powerful of the angels in the Gemini Star mission to clearly indicate that this heavenly mission to earth in no laughing matter.

Angel Love provides Fury with the knowledge and assurance that humanity is gifted with love in all manner; that man cannot help but to embrace love and understanding in the end; that man will prove he can understand God's modern reasoning by accepting the primary purpose of the mission, which is to prevent future conflict in the name of the Lord.

Through her character, angel Love delivers the knowledge and enables the understanding of the modern commandment. Every man's duty to God and heaven is to help prevent the persecution and suffering of his fellow man. Meek and powerful alike share in the understanding that God hears prayers and that He suffers in knowing life on earth is not always pleasant; His answer to the many prayers is to send and establish the modern commandment; to ask man himself to prevent persecution and suffering, and to rely on the rule of law for most other things that can more easily be codified within written laws and common agreement. These are things you already know; heaven likes to encourage good things; angels like to provide good messages.

To spread the rule of law, and its enforcement, is to help spread love and happiness by increasing safety and well being. Safety ensures families grow together in love and happiness, and that persecution and suffering are kept to a minimum within the community. The rule of law, and its honest enforcement, enables business to develop and business means jobs, and that is what man really needs. With business and jobs, love can prosper, and the angel and God can rest a little easier knowing love spreads across the entire world by way of peaceful existence.

These words are not happy-go-lucky ideas, nor are they written out of joy; this is heaven reaching into the world to help you understand that you can and should answer your own prayers; God gave you the tools to help one another. There are modern cities, and there are ancient cities; all cities can work together by communicating clearly; that is heavenly purpose delivered into the world.

Some of you have smart phones; some of you have no food; some of the innocent are experiencing terror, even dying; that is gospel, and gospel is sometimes tragic. You value the life of a God-fearing soldier bound for heaven, in place of the poor child caught in war and terror he did not create; it is the starving child who seems destined to arrive at the gates of heaven ahead of the soldier, who was capable of creating his own destiny. Ask yourself what love is, and what the purpose of sacrifice is; know that fighting for love in the defense of the innocent is a worthy cause in the name of heaven and humanity, and brings us closer. God has always honored worthy soldiers with the offer of life; though heaven is an attractive offer when you see the light through the gates of heaven.

Love whomever you want and just don't break the law; no longer imagine God was ever naïve regarding desire and passion. There is no reason in hiding from God in shyness; He knows wellbeing; He is the master of wellbeing, follow your heart into wellbeing, and do not squander love; He and the angels, along with your own eternal being, may have helped bring the love you found.

Man is adult now and capable of making his personal choices, and following his own heart; your choices are to encourage love and to appreciate love; your choice does not include speaking for God and heaven in judgment.

Love God, praise God, fear God; speak for yourself regarding your concerns over love, or the lack of love in the world; spread the gospel and spread His love assertively.

It is His intent to encourage wellbeing in an assertive manner; His love is not passive; do not accept the natural desire for wellbeing any more passively than you reach for love; do not imagine that romantic love, love for your family and friends, and love of God, are anymore important than your love for the child who is hungry, and ducking for cover. Your passive commitment to your neighbor across the world who died from starvation was just not enough commitment to answer that prayer for life. God was concerned enough over humanity's perception of heavenly passivity that He sent a whole earthly mission to make sure mankind got the message.

God is the shepherd of humanity on Earth; there are worlds in the universe dying over love; God has greater things to be concerned with than monitoring a right and wrong way to love. The important thing is to recognize love, and what it can do for your wellbeing. Your wellbeing is not a casual thing or after thought of existence; God asks you to come back to Him healthy, and in good mind. There is no requirement for a good clean mind and healthy being; these are only helpful things leading you toward heavenly progress both in life, and in eternity. Resources are resources both in life and in death; use your resources wisely in life and ensure we all benefit eternally.

Consider what is sacred; understand God and His plans are sacred. His story of man and heaven together are the sacred thing existing between us forever. The life you see and understand now is no more sacred than the eternal life of your being that you cannot fully know now.

The commandment is to prevent persecution and suffering wherever it is found. Heaven knows and feels persecution and suffering of the living, and the dying. There is only goodness in easing suffering, and paving the simple path to eternal salvation; sounds too easy to be true, and it sounds like wishful thinking. Dying does not need to be complicated; decisions to avoid suffering are personal; heaven is prepared when you are; it's that simple.

Love God, praise God, fear God; love more; encourage less pain.

There has always been enough pain in the world; do not suffer added pain considering heaven and God needed or intended to complicate already complicated decisions over life and death that are very personal in nature, and yours to make, and to live with.

Life includes the burden of considering things; consider these things carefully, and understand that as adults, you have a sacred duty to consider these words, and know they are not sent lightly. Consideration is good; acceptance is yours to decide on; practice is your freedom; your sacred duty is to honor the innocent heart, and recognize an open heart.

There are well known oceans of love in the world; there are only small streams of hate. There is no doubting the power of love; there is no reason to consider anything other than your own loving duty, when you must make hard decisions regarding life and death; heaven is ready; God already knows, and has always been ready and waiting.

Angel Love is a heavenly daughter of the emotion family of angels living now in mortal life. In 2016 she is still young enough to deliver the gospel's hope for a child of the epoch; that light of possibility will fade in a few short years, and that path will close. Real time prophecy is a rare thing to grasp and shape; history is yours to embrace and create while the book of fate remains open and unwritten. There is time enough still; but mankind would necessarily need to be united, intelligent, and on time. The question is: is there enough love and togetherness in the world to deliver the admitted grand child of the epoch. That is the bold and brave thing to consider when you consider sacred Love.

I have known for several years that an added child of prophecy would be named Matthew Zachary, and inherit my natural surname as his also. On October 8, 2016 the final proofing of this story will be complete. Redemption has completed her initial reading; she will read it again several times, because she is he kindest of women and wonderful. The story will pass today to Faith for editing. As I write these words there is a massive hurricane within a few hundred miles of our house. The storm is slowly grinding its way north embroiling the east coast in turmoil; the hurricane is named Matthew. It is a coincidence that on the very day this story passes to angel Faith for editing; nature offers a storm of historic proportions, and man names it Matthew; details like this are not for ignoring when the offering of detail seems intentional for the sake of the completeness of the story. Fury enjoys God's hand on his shoulder, and would never shrug off any heavenly reassurance. Of course, Matthew Zachary will only work if the child is a boy; Love long ago anticipated the boy. I only include the prophetic detail of the hurricane in passing, because the detail seems to be heaven sent, and appropriate for the story.

SECTION XII

Angel Doubt

THE PRIMARY PURPOSE OF <u>THE GOSPEL OF FURY</u> IS NOT THE PATH to God, and the Kingdom of Light; we will all get there sooner or later, and that is a foregone conclusion.

The power of light and the power of being are gifts we are still only beginning to explore through our ever increasing view of a universe we can not fully know, but can imagine. The highways to God are the multilane highways of life filled with bridges, overpasses and connections that have always been well travelled by all souls; those paths are diverse and are yours to maintain, and are yours to freely explore. <u>The Gospel of Fury,</u> and the Gemini Star mission, deliver God's path into the world of today and tomorrow to shape the future that must be planned for. It is sacred duty to know the shepherd makes plans, necessarily including plans for man.

We cannot fully know the future of humanity, and we cannot fully understand the goodness the shepherd must plan for. We can easily see, and readily agree, that He has made provisions for our insight through the understandable message, and verifiable stars and keys He provides. This story clearly demonstrates some of the tools of creation He can use to tell His story, and also lays the skeleton for the future of His message. Do not imagine that God and heaven ever planned for their message and purpose to remain in the past, or that this gospel is the final word, or that the vast future will be denied His provision for continual insight and direction.

Angel Doubt is the twelfth angel of the mission for the epoch, and the fourth member of the close family core of the Gemini Star. Doubt has always been my cousin, and has been my brother-in-law since I married his sister angel Redemption in 1995. Doubt was born on 09/15/1977. Doubt is a Virgo according to the Zodiac, and the outlier of the close family core of messengers identified for the mission as Gemini. A child conceived on September 15th of any given year will likely be born nine months later as a Gemini, and will fulfill the great aspirations of the Gemini Star mission as described in the gospel.

As you can imagine, at this point in the story Doubt is faced with a mortal life that lacks too much doubt. Doubt's duty in heaven is to assist God, and all heavenly beings, with questions and concerns relating to doubt. Doubt about love; doubt about God; all inclusive doubt in general! Angel Doubt has a greater role, which is to monitor doubt in the world so that oblivion does not gain ground on humanity. Doubt's mortal life is based in confidence and well being; he usually has a great time at everything he is involved in. Doubt is a joy to be around, a clever thinker, and he is fairly spiritual; he feels the tug of his eternal being reminding him of great purpose. (I just get tickled knowing the truth of the gospel.)

Doubt is a healthy form of skepticism, and skepticism is a good thing. To question God's purpose, to question God's existence, to question eternal being; these are healthy things to ponder, and to ponder is to avoid oblivion. To live in oblivion is to live with an empty heart closed to imagination, and closed to the possibility of the greater purpose of our shared universe. It is only oblivion that is the scourge of being.

Try not to arrive oblivious when you arrive at the gates of heaven; you risk a shattered soul; though you will be repaired, you will cause a delay at the gates of heaven.

Doubt in goodness is a two way street. You may doubt heavenly goodness since this gospel has laid the Apocalypse of God's justice at your feet. You may doubt God's own goodness, and place blame when things in your life don't appear as nice as you would imagine they should, or could have been. In turn you may doubt humanity's goodness, since injustice and harm are often perceived as rampant in the world. Doubt is a good thing when it is maintained; and only a bad thing when it is out of control.

Angel Doubt provides the archangel with the simple warning to be aware of man's penchant to doubt God's goodness, and to question His purpose; holding God accountable for all the bad things that happen seems prevalent sometimes. "How could God let that happen," is one of man's favorite statements; we have all heard that one, and may have used it ourselves.

Goodness is relative to understanding natural existence; embracing goodness includes understanding the nature of life including the spiritual value of karma, and in accepting possibilities that exist in mystery. Love is a good thing and hate is a bad thing is not true; life is good and death is bad is not true; maintaining the nature of all things is good and necessary; wisdom includes knowing that all of the natural things that exist are necessary things, and there is simpler success in life when we embrace the good and the bad knowing that mystery is real, and that there is fresh purpose around every corner.

Life is a temporal existence along a path filled with twists and turns that contain risk and reward, based on what we see and know as happiness and sadness; true goodness removes any doubt that the promise of life ever included anything but suffering. If your neighbor is hungry, and you are fed; who suffers and who lives in goodness? When children die in war, and soldiers live, who suffers, and who lives in goodness? Life is life and full of questions; there is salvation, and that is God's promise; so in the end there is goodness for all, and that is plain and simple.

Doubting God's existence is not a bad thing if you also leave your heart open to His possibility; He will make His way in sooner or later. You can doubt goodness, but you cannot doubt the presence of His word and promise; accepting the Shepherd's modern word is to accept the presence of the greater path, and the future that must be planned for, and will be shaped according to desire; His promise is ours to inherit.

God's goodness can exist in doubt, and remain questionable when we consider the value of life, and misunderstand eternal purpose. There exists the very real need to prove eternal presence for the questions life has to have answered, and so that heaven receives its return from life through the power and magic of belief; sharing is caring for heaven and earth.

When we mention Interstellar, we mention a great movie released in 2014. A portion of the movie demonstrates eternal being seeking to make its presence known in the reality of life. The notion of interstellar admits understanding and recognition that mortal coincidence can exist to make us cognizant of heaven and purpose, to encourage man to behold God's great power within His universe. Only once in a while does gospel need to come along to provide this level of progressive detail in order to reassure man that his journey and his belief do make the difference. The facts of our lives are God's stars and keys, and we admit them with a knowing wink and a nod, and call it interstellar.

There is a child buried somewhere in the Alaskan tundra who was born May 29th, and who passed June 3rd. We know the child only lived long enough to attain two or three years of age. May 29th is the day Redemption was born, and June 3rd is the day that Fury was born. The child's birth date and death date exist in coincidence with our two birthdates, and rises as very real spiritual presence, albeit very sad spiritual presence, that cannot to be ignored and avoided.

It may be alarming and even discomforting to know and understand that there would be interstellar activity intended to bring two messengers closer together in mortal knowledge, but require the sacrifice of a child's life. Then again, we are speaking to purpose that is designed to convince all of humanity that may face doubt, in His true global intent and purpose. Again, doubt in goodness is one thing; doubt in the reality of God is pointless, when the gospel presents compelling evidence for the progressive world of modern man.

Coincidence rises to the level of miracle when it needs to serve the whole of humanity; coincidence can be large or small when it is relevant, and is presented within the gospel as miracle. We must knowingly accept the sacrifice of the child's life out of respect for heaven and earth, and the reality of this mission and story. Being thankful for the sacrifice of life misrepresents the truth, the family, and heaven. The child lived and died years before the television story exposed any reality of coincidence that could be used to establish heavenly purpose; just as the world wars existed long before any link to heavenly justice was explained; it is easier to put the horse in front of the cart when the cart is empty, and we are looking backward. The child rests now with God in faith and in love, regardless of the news being shared in our story. We can assure the parents that the gospel serves God, and all of humanity; admittedly it was no small sacrifice, and will not be forgotten or overlooked. Pilgrimage and enshrinement are very real things, and exist as truth, tested in our time on earth.

We sat closely in our bedroom channel surfing, stopping at what may have been the Discovery Channel, and a series whose subject was man's survival in the wilds of Alaska. Not something we would usually watch. A father was telling his story of survival, including the harrowing tale of their loss of a beloved youngster who wandered off, and subsequently drowns in a shallow pool of water. The television program shows the burial marker clearly labeled with the date of birth May 29, and date of passing June 3. Her birthday and my birthday together on one grave marker; this seems highly improbable, and quite a coincidence; I wonder what the odds are. The fact that we shared the coincidence, and even saw that program, is significant and interstellar. We witnessed the show together sometime in 2015, while truth was still creating understanding that would connect belief to facts that would translate into God's progressive evidence for this real story.

We bowed our heads together in knowing, and in grievance over the loss of the child's life. Leaving the child out of this gospel, and out of our lives, and your life, was not a possibility. When we receive God's word through an interstellar message that demonstrates probability and may increase knowing, then you must pass on the message to help keep doubt at bay. There are important possibilities at stake for life, and the future, so the gospel must remain compelling in order to get us close to reaching heavenly intent; close is good enough for horseshoes and hand grenades, and for getting rid of just enough doubt, which is all we really needed.

PART THREE

The Parables of Fury

SECTION I

The Parable of the Anti-Christ

THE PATH THROUGH CREATION TO MAN IS THE PATH GOD USES; OUR path from life to salvation is the path He promises. The Lord claims creation boldly through His design and intelligence; He provides us His evidence in the verifiable life, and true story of Fury. Born 06/03/63, Fury saw God provide the star of creations birthday; Fury combines the date 6363 to come up with 666 the number of the biblical beast; not in jest nor in worry, but in proof does the number of the beast fall into place to unlock God's biblical mystery, and solidify today's gospel story into fact.

God uses what He chooses out of love and possibility; to demonstrate intent and purpose with fact based evidence so that His design and intelligence can be witnessed in the one life of angel Fury. The fact-based evidence combined with the words of the story, present the gospel in a believable form so that the modern work may be examined and authenticated. There are things in the modern gospel mankind must accept and use; the modern gospel must be maintained.

Fury admits during his lifetime that he is not Christ; therefore he is anti-Christ. Christ is the son of God, who lived a real life two-thousand years ago. The son of God passed through creation on a mission to deliver the guarantee of forgiveness along with the promise of salvation. Forgiveness and salvation belong now to man through the love of the Father and through the love of the son. The son of God lived a mortal life, and was returned to the Father. The son of God has provided his Father both the living legacy, and the heavenly existence; the son is whole in the eyes of heaven, and in the eyes of the earth; the promises of the Father and the son include all of humanity for all of time without condition; that is the bond that exists between Father and son.

Fury is but a simple messenger sent to clear things up through simplicity, and to provide the modern gospel so that mankind may receive His modern touch and know He loves us still.

SECTION II

The Parable of the Arc of the Covenant

THERE IS A COVENANT THAT GOD MAINTAINS WITH MAN. THE covenant takes a faith based path from God through the archangel Fury at the passage of the First Epoch of Humanity into the Second Epoch of Humanity. The covenant that God maintains with man is that man is good enough. The covenant may sound simplistic, and of not much value, but often those things that appear to have small value turn out to be highly valuable.

Fury is the carrier of the covenant, and is therefore the Arc of the Covenant. The covenant that God maintains with man will remain yours in faith alone for now. Time will uncover the fuller extent of the value of the covenant. The Shepherd's journey with man is still just beginning; Apocalyptic fears of Armageddon and the destruction of the jewel of Earth are overblown ideas arising from man's impressive progress in recent years. Don't be too disappointed to know that man's future with God is a foregone conclusion; He won't leave you alone.

SECTION III

The Parable of an Epoch of Humanity

IN 2016 THERE HAS BEEN TWO-THOUSAND YEARS OF HUMANITY'S history that have passed since the son of God walked the earth. It is no accident that the modern testament arrives at this time in history. The celebration and acknowledgement of the epoch are recorded in this modern gospel. An epoch is two thousand years of mankind's history; the heavenly equivalent to that is one month. One mortal lifetime, or about seventy-five years, is the equal of one heavenly day.

Imagine the earth and man in eleven more epochs, which will be one heavenly year from when the son first walked the earth which will be twenty-two thousand years from now give or take. Talk about the possibility of the destruction of the planet over twenty-two thousand years; then you have reason to worry; do not imagine God and heaven will be left out of mankind's story; be prepared for the gospel and look for it and plan for it; it will come as plainly and clearly as this story comes to you now.

Praise God, Love God, Fear God; be on the look out for the word of God; it will come again and again.

SECTION IV

The Parable of the Gemini Star

GOD PROVIDED A STAR FOR TODAY'S MISSION TO EARTH. HE designed the recognizable mission around the Zodiac and used the symbol of the Gemini twins to insure His design and intelligence would shine through from creation so that the story would be a success. Without stars we will have more difficulty recognizing the keys to unlock God's mystery.

On May 26, 1966 God, and an angel on earth, brought twin Gemini girls into the world of mankind. The twin daughters of heaven's creation are combined forever with another angel on earth born exactly three years later on May 26, 1969. Together theses acts of creation exist to symbolize the Gemini Star which shines brightly for the world and represents God's modern mission.

The facts of the births are verifiable, and proudly show us God's power through His design and intelligence and that He will use creation as He sees fit to shape the future of humanity. His great power over creation is both individual and generational. He can shape a life and He can shape entire generations of people. God's power over humanity is greater than we can imagine.

SECTION V

The Parable at the Heart of the Sun

SINCE ANGEL FURY WAS A BOY, GOD HAS BEEN GENTLY WHISPERING His plans. God delivered Fury with an affinity for the Sun. Being is real; beings must have rest on earth as they do in heaven; all being has a resting place whether it be a bed, or object, or belief. Fury is honored as the Being at the Heart of the Sun. This you may take on faith, and also know that the story supports the underlying message, and the importance behind the reasoning.

The Sun is the center of our galaxy, and provides the earth with the nourishing energy that causes life to proliferate. Life is the ultimate purpose of God, and life is what gives God meaning and purpose. The Sun is our star. The Sun touches all of us daily; the universe supports our lives continually; all humanity exists as a result of perfect planning, or accidental circumstance. When accidents lead to something as perfect as our creation, we can be thankful that God is there to help us explain it all, and to shepherd us along a path that would otherwise be lonely in a universe where we are just a small spec.

Praise God, love God, fear God; do not be lonely; He is with us in progress.

SECTION VI

The Parable of the Apocalypse

GOD'S GENERATIONAL POWER OVER CREATION AND HUMANITY IS not to be underestimated, ignored or misunderstood. There is a path in this gospel that we must follow. He ensures we understand the things He will not accept by ensuring His word is received by mankind. He ensures His word is delivered by cleverly crafting His mission, and sending vital things that skeptics can examine so that understanding can be reached. The knowledge the gospel provides is clear; do not place blame onto God's shoulders when it belongs on the shoulders of men.

The future will not include wars in God's name, or in the name of his religions. Crimes committed in God's name are unholy, and the consequences rest on the shoulders of individuals. Individuals experience Judgment Day in heaven. Do not be so daft as to commit crimes in life that will result in God participating in your personal judgment. Commit crimes in your name alone, and fight your wars in your own names; do not fight wars in the name of God, or contribute to religious persecution in the name of God.

The Apocalyptic justice that is described in this gospel is real; mankind's en masse forgiveness for all trespass that exists previously, is real. You may uncover history, and reconcile much destruction of the past, to discover that time after time destruction has been accredited to God in order to spread spiritual word, practice, and belief; do not imagine that

God is so petty as to require destruction of life to spread gospel. Placing blame upon God for killing in order to spread gospel would not stand; The Gospel of Fury admits that the hammers of judgment restore the balance between heaven and earth, and that humanity's redemption has been attained.

SECTION VII

The Parable of the Fallen Angel

GOD ENABLED HIS BIBLICAL TRUTH ALONG WITH POPULAR character references from spiritual story telling to fall within grasp of the life of messenger Fury. The purpose of popular character reference is to create understanding, enhance awareness, and to spread the gospel by increasing interest and speculation as to the possibility that God would send His modern message, or not.

The reason for pursuing popularity is to maximize reach, and encourage dissemination. Achieving the maximum potential spread of the gospel will allow the archangel to increase the happiness of the Father, the glory of heaven, and the success of humanity.

The gospel contains character references including the presence of the anti-Christ on earth, the finding of the Holy Grail, the second coming of the son-of-God, and the Arc of the Covenant in order to enhance the complexity of the story, and to create intrigue. Archangel Fury can add to these claims of fame by painting awareness that he understands he can be described as being the Fallen Angel who betrays secrets belonging to the Kingdom of Heaven.

The cynical approach toward analyzing Fury and the message within these gospel words may describe a loose angel who sneaks out of heaven with a plan to deceive the world, and trick humanity into betraying some of its long held traditions. The skeptic, though, will know and understand that it is unlikely that an angel who serves God by design would actually consider sneaking out through God's Rainbow of Creation just to obtain life for a brief moment of time. The truth is that the archangel serves God on the side of heavenly justice, and that whether or not the archangel wins or loses in life, God still wins in the end as long as the gospel is maintained for humanity.

Love Him, Praise Him, Fear Him; do not lose or manipulate His words again.

SECTION VIII

The Parable of Earthly Legacy

HEAVEN EXISTS AND THE EARTH EXISTS; THE CLOSER TOGETHER they exist the closer in harmony they exist. The closer to one another they exist, the higher degree of harmony can be reached. In other words, when heaven and earth see eye to eye, things are good.

Being that exists in heaven is heavenly being; heavenly being alone is not the fullest potential of being; some things that are to be must reach the highest level of being in order to achieve the highest heavenly regard. The son-of-God exists within heaven in eternity prior to his earthly mission, and after his earthly mission following his departure out of the mortal world of time; his earthly legacy is a badge of courage, and lends itself to his understanding of the world, and the suffering life has a tendency to provide. An easier way of speaking to the relevance of earthly legacy is to admit that your heavenly existence gains more credibility if your heavenly self makes a trip into the world of man and actually lives a life.

To become a heavenly being that is supported in known earthly legacy is a goal of a higher order. To acknowledge and then reach for that goal which is desired and described to you is, on the one hand, to understand and admit to the reality of the heavenly goal, which is a step in the right direction and, on the other hand, have the opportunity to serve God directly; make Him smile now, while these things are so plainly given to you, and deliver happiness between heaven and earth and deliver God His legacy.

God creates and describes what He wants; those things He wants are what you want. If Fury tells you God wants a grandchild then believe it, or not, but write your decision into the book of fate willingly and knowingly. Destiny is not quite within sight, and the future is not known.

SECTION IX

The Parable of the Stars

THE BONES OF CREATION ARE THE DATES OF OUR DELIVERY, AND the dates of our passing. These are some of the tools God can use to demonstrate His message. These dates are called stars, and when they serve to unlock mystery they become keys to spiritual existence and learning. The keys are the skeletons of creation, and create the paths we use into knowing the things God needs us to know.

God's stars that become clear keys to unlock His mystery are rare things. There are many rare things provided in this gospel to assist us in knowing the reality of His word. It may be a big leap to accept that just one star could demonstrate the onset of God's apocalyptic justice; that just one star could demonstrate the conclusion of the apocalyptic era; that is what He can do, and that is what He did do. It is up to you to accept the gospel, and use God's stars and keys to solve mystery and learn the reality of His experience.

SECTION X

The Parable of the Holy Grail

NOT ONLY SOME OF MANKIND; ALL OF MANKIND, UNCONDITIONALLY and forever; this is how much the son-of-God is devoted to what he loves most; humanity.

Our Father in heaven loves the son; our Father in heaven loves many things. Our Father in heaven is the Father of the perfect universe; planning for perfection does not always translate into a reality that is a foregone conclusion. On many occasions life is suffering; the son-of-God knows this, and his Father recognizes this as well. In agreement, the Father and son hold a sacred bond between them that offers the eternal assurance of peace and happiness.

The Holy Grail of your mortal experience, now and forever, is that bond which exists between the Father and the son. The agreement exists between God and His son that men, women, and children are forgiven for mortal sin and trespass. The eternal agreement acknowledges the imperfection of a life that includes survival, and doing your best to be good.

SECTION XI

The Parable of the Modern Commandment

THE RULE OF LAW AND ITS JUST ADMINISTRATION IS THE GOLDEN element of civilization. The rule of law demonstrates humanity's civilized progress toward societal living that includes goodness and fairness and justice. Not all elements of life can be written into the rule of law as easily as those things that are apparent rights and wrongs.

God hears prayers, and heaven knows He feels the pains of living. The persecuted and the suffering pray loudly, and often, for relief. Those are the payers that are more easily handled by humanity rather than God, who shepherds a world separated by time and creation. The power of eternal being is true power, is a simpler power, a more gentle power. Man is uniquely positioned to know and practice the modern commandment.

We are created in His intellectual image so that we can understand, and so that He can shepherd. He gave us the power of love; He gave us the power to think so that we may create. Mankind is ready now to receive the modern commandment to prevent persecution and suffering.

We appreciate goodness. Goodness means preventing persecution and suffering.

SECTION XII

The Parable of Christ

THERE ARE SUCH THINGS AS SERIOUS SOULS. PASSING FROM eternity through creation to successfully deliver the modern testament requires a serious soul. A serious soul is a soul that has been tested time after time, passing between heaven and earth, serving God and man. Passing between the vast expanses of eternal existence into the mortality of time exacts a large toll on a soul.

A serious messenger has arrived now, and provided you with God's design and creation for our modern time. The messenger has given you many things that God enabled, and these things serve purpose both for man, and for heaven.

By His design it will appear that the archangel of the first epoch of man was indeed the second coming of Christ.

Printed in the United States
By Bookmasters